LET THE FUN BEGIN

By

TERESA QUEEN JOHNSON

Published by
KHA BOOKSELLERS & ASSOCIATES UNLIMITED
26070 Barhams Hill Road - Drewryville, VA 23844
(704) 509-2226 (434) 658-4934

khalifah@khabooks.com – www.khabooks.com

FIRST EDITION - FIRST PRINTING
April 12, 2005

ISBN#1-56411-353-1

YBBG#0349

Printed in the USA by
LUMUMBA BOOK PRINTERS & COMPANY
P. O. Box 9
Drewryville, VA 23844
(704) 509-2226

Book Cover Design by On Target Graphics
1245-104 Kelston Place
Charlotte NC, 28212

CONTENTS

	PAGE
PREFACE	VI
DEDICATION	VIII
INTRODUCTION	IX
TODAY	11
MOLESTATIONS	13
GUILT/VOLUNTEERING	16
SPAGHETTI	20
PLEASING PEOPLE	21
BELIEVING MAMA	22
WHITE WHORE	23
FOCUS ON QUEEN	24
OTHER SPONSORS	26
MOLESTATIONS II	28
SISTER, SISTER	29
NEUROSIS BREAK	32
JOB HUNTING	33
AUNTIE RUTH	34
THE MAN	36
ANNETTE	37
STRATEGIES	38
REPETITION	39
FASHION SHOW	40
UNCLE WILLIAM	43
NANA AND BUTCH	46
NORMALCY?	48
FRIENDS?	50
HATE	52
GWEN W.	53
LIVE	54
SHOPPING	55
CHARLES' SISTER	56
DOLLS AND BREASTS	57
ONE-EYED MAN	59

ILLEGITIMACY	61
?'S & EXCUSES	63
HAIRY, SCARRY	68
BIG TIME	71
BITCH MILDRED	73
SHOOTING SPREE	75
JAMES	78
RAMBLINGS	80
JAIL	83
THE ICEMAN	86
BARBARA	90
ACCEPTANCE	92
SISTER ANN	95
THE SIXTH FLOOR	97
CONTEMPLATION	100
WORLD IN PALMS	103
FOOT SOLDIERS	105
SUPERFICIAL FAKES	106
CINDERELLA, RELLA-CINDER	109
ALLEY B.	112
REBUILDING	115
HOMECOMING	116
MORE JAMES	116
1ST OMVI	118
HELLFIRE & STONEBRIM	119
DEBACLE	122
PARKSIDE NEIGHBORS	125
NEW QUARTERS	127
THE SHOOTING	129
PILLS, PILLS, PILLS	133
I GIVE	134
CONTRIBUTIONS	135
KIDS	136

THE PIMP   139
RETURN TO DAYTON   143
SCHOOL PROM   145
THE ISLEYS   147
DRUG DOCTORS   150
HOSTAGES   151
MENSTRUATION   152
SPEAK NO EVIL   154
BELIEVING   156
GUSSIE & WHISTLING   157
AGE SIX   159
CHILD RAPISTS   160
FEAR   162
GLORIA   163
EPILOGUE   165

PREFACE

This writing is a challenge, horror, and honor. Millions of people have dedicated their lives, to finding a lasting solution to this revolting illness. Yet everyday, throughout this great land, booze and dope addiction destroys brilliant minds, families, careers and innocent lives. America has the finest treatment facilities in the world.

"How can people harm themselves that way," you ask? Why are they constantly placing themselves in jeopardy and peril? Why don't they get help? It is against this backdrop, I present short and snappy excerpts from my story. I'm living sober proof, that alcoholism and drug addiction can be arrested. Today, I look back with the intention of moving forward. My objective is recovery not regret. I no longer apologize for my former beastly behaviors. The terrors, which bond themselves to alcoholism and drug abuse, are tremendous and severe. My solution involves a physical, psychological and spiritual overhaul. Some of the answers lie within these pages.

To admit I was out of control would be a gross understatement. For twenty-plus years, I drank and took a hodgepodge of legal and illegal drugs. This occurred in spite of home, family, school, church, good moral suasion, law enforcement or any other societal safeguard against "injudiciousness." When I'd "come to" after a night of blacked-out barbarism, I'd feel myself, checking to make sure body parts were whole and still attached. I'd count my breasts, fingers and toes. I would feel my vagina and smell my fingers in an effort to detect traces of "blackout" intercourse. Nobody could tell me anything. All they could do was point in the direction of the bottle, crack pipe, powder or pill. I'd take it from there.

All and I mean all of my plans, drives, goals and

dreams, took a backseat to my drunkenness and drug habit. I worshipped the bottle most of all. I aborted innocent babies, sacrificed family, job community standing and most importantly, my self-respect.

If you are a boozer and junkie, this book is for you. If you're in love with one, this book is definitely for you. I've pulled no punches nor hid any skeletons. It's all here. It's here, waiting for you to process and use. Take what you want and need. As the sober days add up, a happier, exhilarating and more exciting life will be yours. You just have to work for it. There is a way out of the maze.

DEDICATION

This writing is dedicated to the sacred ancestors, whose names I'll never know, but whose spirits guide my every step. It is also my way of saying I love you to a very, very, sick and sad woman- my deceased mother, Wilma Jenny Johnson.

INTRODUCTION

This is a wonderful book. It's about facing oneself and learning to like the results. It can help us resolve many of our perceived concerns about life and happiness. This book covers the early years of my sobriety. It sheds light on my neurosis and various coping mechanisms I used to remain sober. In many places, this writing is crazy, incoherent and detached- just like alcoholism. My last booze and dope debacle occurred on October 13, 1991. The following day, I sought help in a well known twelve step program. Thank you Higher Power!

This writing is for people whose feelings have been deeply, deeply hurt. It's about people who live their lives amid chaos and desperation. It's about people who are in love with drunks and junkies. It's about blameless children and how addiction affects them. Last, but far from least, this book is about learning how to live without booze and dope -one day at a time.

I believe drunks and junkies are spiritually sick. We alcoholics were sick years before choosing booze and dope as escape hatches. After a drinking catastrophe, my pain resurfaced more relentless than ever. This is because true alcoholics and junkies live in searing emotional pain.

There is a way out. There is greatness and power within you. This love offering takes into account room for your thoughts. What are they? Write them down. Use additional paper as needed. As you read and digest this book, record your thoughts and review them often. They are the keys to freedom. Keep your writings in a safe, sacred place. Your writings along with this book are guaranteed to provide assistance with your healing process. Swallow your ego and follow these uncomplicated activities, strategies and suggestions. The first step in mending is admitting there is a dilemma. **In this country, alcoholism** is a **huge problem.** Look at the devastating toll booze and dope extracts from the nation. This great country needs our social, emotional, intellectual, spiritual, financial, and physical contributions. With the help of our Higher Power, we will remain sober one day at a time. In America, help is as near as we want it. Let's work through this madness together. **Let the fun begin!**

Queen

LET THE FUN BEGIN!

TODAY
10/16/94

I sit in this meeting and my mind is wandering all over the place. This country is so "look" conscious, even when the messenger is ugly, concentrate on the message. Even if I disagree with the philosophy of the messenger, its kind to just listen. Sometimes, I don't want to help. Yet, many sober drunks have helped me. Oh my God, when will the neurosis end? Here it comes.

In January 1993, Dayton Daily News was once again filling space with negative information about the "projects." I wrote the newspaper. I shared some of my accomplishments while living in the projects. "Come and interview me" was my challenge to the newspaper. They did! I was shocked.

There's a new Lincoln Continental parked in my driveway. This three-bedroom home with its plush carpet and state of the art kitchen also belongs to me. Creditors extend my credit by thousands of dollars, with only a phone call. I'm well invested. As a matter of fact, my assets have required a second visit from my financial planner. He wants me to take a second look at private penitentiary stocks. Afterall, that's where many drunks and dope fiends call home-or will call home. My man is handsome, strong, kind, loves and listens to me. I'm now respected in the community where I live and work. My body is beautiful because I take care of it. I'm sober today. Thanks Higher Power for your grace.

This is a beautiful country. In most areas of the world, July 10th is a hot summer day. On this day, in 1954, I made my entrance into the vast world of southern segregation. I was born in Tuskegee, Alabama. I was born at John A. Andrews VA Hospital. My mama wasn't married. She worked as a laundress at the hospital. Time to purge the psyche; if I am to remain sober on a daily basis I must become willing to accept a power greater than Queen.

The late great Booker T. Washington and Dr. George Washington Carver are responsible for Tuskegee being on the map. Booker T. Washington founded Tuskegee Institute, now Tuskegee University. I prefer to call it Tuskegee Institute. I guess it's the stubborn streak in me. Dr. Carver was one of the world's greatest scientists. He saved the south from the boll weevil. Dr. Carver was a professor for over forty years at the Institute.

This Higher Power works through me. It's spirituality. The prospect of daily sobriety comes without compromise. Emotional honesty cannot be a mockery of the soul. The soul will allow no such animal as "mockery." It will retaliate. Emotional honesty is the key to daily sobriety. Emotional honesty means acknowledging our feelings-good and otherwise. Honesty comes through realizing one's powerlessness over people, places and things.

Willingness? Am I willing to go to any length to stay sober? I was to get drunk and high. I stalked booze and dope like a vulture hunting for carrion. I walked. I hitchhiked. I sold my ass for booze and dope. What price am I willing to pay for sobriety today? Sobriety is the link between me and my Higher Power.

The serenity prayer works for me. Where did the hatred for the size of my breasts stem from? Why am I willing to invest in plastic surgery and breast development subliminals to rectify another perceived inadequacy in Queen?

I know where the hatred is rooted. The childhood sexual abuse at the hands of Lamar, Andrew and other men is part of it. The brutalizing of my mother by Willie B. Gilmore is another part. The verbal and physical abuse of my aunts by their husbands and lovers are pieces of the puzzle. The workhorse days I spent in the cotton fields of Tuskegee. The biggest piece of the puzzle is the motherwhore of the others. I t was slavery and her afterbirth-segregation.

It's affect upon the entire process of feminization is embedded in my psyche. Embedded in my conscious and subconscious are forces which seek to destroy me.
These forces want to again destroy my home, talents and creative gifts from God. For a drunk like me, the only solution is sobriety. It is only through sobriety that I'm learning to nurture myself on a daily basis. I want this new miraculous life. I'll die a sinister bloody, lonely, pissy death without it.

All who hurt me must be forgiven. The forgiveness process takes place through prayer and meditation. It doesn't happen all at once. Oh the agony! Why should I forgive the rapist, woman beaters and criminals? They hurt me. It still hurts inside. Why must I forgive them? They drove my poor mama to suicide and an early grave. Why should I forgive them? Why?

In order to maintain sobriety, I'm learning to let go of the hurt. By giving the "hurt" continuous power, I'm choosing death while still alive. I deserve the best. I owe Queen today. I'll be grateful I was chosen. I am a walking miracle. Only by Grace am I alive and well today. When the hand of recovery reaches out, I am responsible. This means if another suffering drunk or junkie asks for my help, I'm supposed to help. They talk too much in this meeting.

MOLESTATIONS
10/22/94

I started elementary school in Tuskegee, Alabama. Kindergarten and Headstart hadn't been conceived in 1960. I went straight to first grade. How tattered and unkempt I was. What a disheveled six year old. On plenty of occasions, I went to school barefoot, smelly and ragged. My hair was nappy and short from the lack of care.

My southern teachers were the best I've ever known. Mrs. Martin was my first grade teacher. Our classroom was heated by a black pot bellied stove. I vividly remember how cold my classroom was in winter. I sat in front of the room near the stove. Mrs. Martin cared little about the cold. She cared even less about my exterior appearance. My surface trappings were just that. She was an avenging angel. This old, wonderful, loving teacher-lady believed in me - the Teresa Queen which was hidden from mortal eyes. The Teresa Queen only God saw. Mrs. Martin was my first and second grade teacher at Washington Public School in Tuskegee. Today, educators refer to this as "looping."

Write about a teacher who believed in you.

_____

_____

_____

_____

_____

_____

_____

_____

_____

The first of many tragedies struck in the summer of 1962. Mama's drinking, and the domestic violence in our shack had escalated to the point of no return. My mother had recently given birth to her third illegitimate child. This was a married Willie B. Gilmore's second child by my mother. Mama had three children now. She also carried a booze monkey on her back. She was carrying on in a ruthless and irresponsible manner with her lover, Gilmore. All the relatives were talking about her. Instead of heeding their remonstrations, she became worse.

Mama's sister, Thelma and her husband, Lamar were regular visitors to the south during the summer months. Word had reached Brooklyn, their home, informing them of mama's behavior. It so happened, they were in the south in the summer of 1962.

Aunt Thelma liked me, she always has. She asked mama to let her raise me in New York. Aunt Thelma and Lamar seemed so nice. I knew they'd always love and protect me. Ha! Was I in for a "treat!" Shortly after my arrival, in the Big Apple, I was assigned horrible chores. I dusted, cooked, washed, scrubbed and babysat Andrew Jr. It seemed all I did was clean and feel sorry for myself. I was incarcerated within those foul walls.

To add insult to injury, Lamar and Andrew Sr. would sexually molest my eight year old body until it pained continuously. Andrew Sr., Joyce and Andrew Jr. lived on the third floor of 288 Lafayette Avenue. Their wives were young and vibrant. My aunt was in her late thirties. Andrew's wife, Joyce, was in her late teens. They were married to beautiful women. Yet, these two lousy excuses for men would rape me whenever desire and / or opportunity presented itself. This father and son was a frightening child molesting team. I rarely slept while living in that hell house.

The twisted nature of their awful actions caused them tremendous guilt. They knew what they were doing was wicked, dishonest and criminal. Lamar would beat me at the slightest breach. Lamar threatened to kill my mama if I her told about him. My mother died never knowing the terror I endured in Brooklyn, New York. Andrew seemed to idolize me more with each assault. He would shower me with sweets. Because my drunken mother was incapable of caring for me, as an innocent child, I was caught between two psychotic dicks. Alcoholism is a bitch!

It was in Brooklyn, New York that these soul robberies took place. It was in Brooklyn that the loneliness and depression I wrestle with to this day set in. The black depression with its companion listlessness, were my childhood consorts. I remember no childhood friends in New York, only fighting during or after school and boundless unhappiness.

Thank you Higher Power for my sobriety today. It is only through my willingness to accept another power greater than myself that keeps me from booze, dope and suicide. The unconditional love of my Higher Power strengthens me one day at a time. I fully realize that despair, anguish, hate and hurt still reside within my consciousness. My childhood demons are ready and waiting to destroy me. All I have to do is drink and I will die at their grisly hands. God help me! I pray for sanity and relief when thoughts of another binge surface- Higher Power please keep me sober. One day at a time- sobriety just for today. I will trust the process.

GUILT AND VOLUNTEERING
10/23/94

In September of 1994, I volunteered for Miami Valley hospital's candy stripers. I was interviewed on November 11, 1994. The coordinator of the program was a white yuppie type. She told me that she was a former secretary embarking on a new career. No real communication occurred during my interview. We talked about niceties, nothing deep or profound. She suggested I volunteer in the hospital's rehab unit for drunks and junkies. I said "NO!" I'm steering clear of treatment facilities. At the time, I believed such facilities hampered one's recovery from booze and dope.

Again, guilt reared its gory head and I shared my real preference. Since my daughter's birth, I'd been a terribly lousy mother. I wanted to work in the newborn unit. Guilty as charged. For years, my daughter and I have been at odds. I know the culprit was my active alcoholism. Merciless and unrelenting, it tore us apart when she was just a baby. At age fourteen she'd had enough.

Earlier that August 1986 evening, after hours of booze, syrup, pills, crack cocaine and who knows what else, I started playing "bullet machine" with the washer. I began to fire bullets from my Smith and Wesson 38 into my washer. One of the bullets ricocheted off of the washing machine, passed through the wall and narrowly missed my next door neighbor's sleeping two month old baby. The neighbor called the police. This is exactly what she should have done. I was taken to jail. Like an animal, I slept on the cold floor in a colder jail cell.

My daughter placed a frantic long distance call to Cleveland. Several family members resided in this city by the lake. Neither my daughter, sister, nor aunts checked to see whether I was alright when they arrived in Dayton from Cleveland. They picked up my daughter and drove away. That was seven years ago. By God's grace I am able to retell the parts which weren't blacked out. Did I mention I was a black-out drunk? It would be nearly eight years and a great tragedy later before I laid eyes on her again.

The last Saturday morning in January 1995, my sleep was interrupted by a ringing telephone. It was my daughter. At the time she was twenty and the mother of my thirty day old granddaughter. As the curtain of the last year opened, nasty revelations came to the fore.

My only daughter had become heavily involved in prostitution. Her pimp had turned his stable against her- or so she said. This pimp was my grandbaby's father. My daughter was one of his biggest money making whores. "Whore!" What a filthy word. Of all available choices in America, she chose whoredom! Not only that, she fell in love with her pimp. Now, the health of my grandchild depended on his volatile drug dependent whims.

Let's return to this early morning phone call. This was the call I'd longed for over the years. She sounded desperate. Mama's help was finally needed. The wonderful thing about this scenario was I could help her. At long last I could help her! I'd been sober almost four years and my life was going well. I could finally help my whorish daughter. "What do you want to do?" I asked. "Can I come home?" was what I heard from the voice on the other end of the line. Of course you can, where's the baby? Is she alright? "She's here in the apartment with my wife-in-law." A wife-in-law is a slang name for whores in the same stable. "She's fine mama."

As a child, I become accustomed to sleeping on the floor and carried this custom into adulthood. That is exactly where I was during our conversation. I sat up on my mattress-bed. The time to think clearly required a straight firm back. "When do you want to leave?" "As soon as I can, things aren't going as I expected," she said.

My mind was racing. The fastest way to travel was by plane. "Hold on" I said and thanked God. We chose Continental Airlines. The die was cast. At long last, my daughter and granddaughter were coming home. There's a three hour delay between the times zones of Dayton and Los Angeles. Jamessa and I hung up around 4:00a.m. Dayton time. Her flight was due to leave LAX at 7:40 in the morning. My heart was racing. Energy and happiness flooded my being. Take your time, I cautioned myself. Take your time. This is wonderful. I was ecstatic. Finally, after six years of being apart my prodigal daughter was coming home.

Scarcely able to contain my happiness, I must have floated on clouds all morning. Since I didn't have a credit card I drove to the airport, and paid $353.00 for a one way plane ticket to Ohio. I left Cox International in Dayton and drove home on the same cloud. At two o'clock Dayton time, I checked with Continental. I was in the public library and used a pay phone to contact the airline. She had not boarded the flight. The ticket was still at the Continental counter. What happened? Why hadn't she boarded the plane?

After hanging up with Continental and thoroughly disgusted, I called Aunt Lillie. Her name is Lillie Henry Felton. She's my mother, father, sister, brother, friend, confidant, you fill in the rest. She is a godsend. Although unrelated, she's very dear to me. I hope I've made that clear. This wise, old, illiterate lady has more sense in her little toe than most of the great western philosophers combined.

Aunt Lillie said Puddin" (Jamessa's nickname), hadn't called her. She assured me everything would be alright. We hung up. This time I called Continental's 800 numbers. The agent in Denver was really helpful and concerned. She located my daughter at LAX in Los Angeles. Thank goodness! Jamessa went to the Delta counter and thus missed her flight. She said I didn't say Continental was her airline. Anyhow, I said "stay put." I'll wire more money for you and the baby. By this time, she'd missed both flights into Dayton. "You can catch the Sunday morning flight into Dayton" I said. Continental provided her with a hotel voucher. With baby in tow, she checked into the airport Holiday Inn.

Around 5:30 p.m., I wired money to the hotel, via Western Union. By this time, she had a plane ticket, cash money and fine lodging in a top rated establishment. All that was left was for her to eat rest and board the plane for Ohio on Sunday. For a child of an alcoholic mother, that was too simple. It was too rational, too easy. By her nature, she had to complicate matters and clutter my best laid plans.

Jamessa checked out of the hotel in the wee hours of the morning and slithered back to her pimp. My daughter consciously returned to the hell of whoredom and abuse. Like my drinking and drugging, that lifestyle was the comfort zone she'd grown to accept. She didn't even cash in the plane ticket. I'll pray for them.

On April 29, 1996, Jasmine Charlene Johnson, my granddaughter, choked to death on a piece of hotdog meat. She was sixteen months young. God kept me sober.
How did we get off into that-WOW?! Oh yes, the coordinator for the volunteer candy stripers at the hospital lied to me. She said, she'd call and give me a schedule. It's a good thing I didn't hold my breath. The past is over and I will make the memories work in my favor. Today I realize I was vicariously struggling to mother both my daughter and my newborn grandbaby. I felt so guilty.

SPAGHETTI
10-23-94

Charles is my friend and lover. Sexually, I should have left him alone. Our likes and dislikes are similar. We both enjoy delicious, well prepared food. Try this delicious spaghetti concoction when you prioritize a couple of hours for kitchen duty.

Brown meat and drain. Combine everything except spaghetti in large pot, preferably cast iron. Simmer ingredients for sixty to ninety minutes. Boil spaghetti until fork tender. This takes around eight to ten minutes. Serve with sauce on top of spaghetti or mixed together. Garnish with your favorite cheese topping. My personal favorite is sharp cheddar. Enjoy with garlic bread and your favorite beverage. If you're an alcoholic stick to soda, milk, water, juice, tea or coffee.

• Spaghetti	• Garlic powder (2 heaping tablespoons)
• Spaghetti mushroom mix (two packs)	• Garlic bread
• Mushrooms (large can)	• Ground chuck (I pound)
• Oregano (1/2 teaspoon)	•Italian sausage (1 pound)
• Tomatoes (crushed large can)	• Cheese topping
• Green pepper	• Salt / pepper to taste

PLEASING PEOPLE
10/24/94

Which concerns do I wish to resolve right now? Today, I'll ground myself in the belief that my Higher Power loves me and is taking care of me. What sorts of consequences are necessary in order for me to appreciate my myriad of gifts? None! On a daily basis, I'm learning to rid myself of the subconscious desire to harm and defeat myself. That's better, "Gratitude is important." What do I do with my blessings in sobriety? I share them!

This people pleasing is so deeply entrenched within me. It stems from trying to make my crazy mama love me. I'm over forty years young. Why am I still enslaved by the confused inner child? Do I fear rejection that much? I have to walk through the fear. I'm destined to become the world's greatest sober alcoholic. Let them laugh. Laughter is healthy.

I have a responsibility to myself. Sharing my sober gifts via speaking and writing is my job. It's my life's work. To listen and share with others is important to me.

Why did you drink so much? Was it conditioning, values or sociocultural factors? They all played a part. Mostly the above excuses are just a stinking batch of cow manure. I drank because it felt good. The effect booze produced was magical. What a wonderful elixir, if one isn't alcoholic or addicted. Drunks and dope fiends are our own worst enemies. That's why the obsession for sobriety has to become more powerful than the booze/dope obsession. Like I shared earlier, booze was my God. Alcohol ruled my life. John Barleycorn was king of the hill. Wow! It led to other drugs. That's heavy. Here I am sober and learning to live in the "now." Who's responsible? Whose life is this anyway? That's right-it's mine.

BELIEVING MAMA
11/14/94

It's time to shop for groceries. I placed my car in the shop for a transmission tune-up today. There's a star search audition at Memorial Hall this evening. I thought, why not attend and tryout. Well, I've always wanted to be a movie star, singer and entertainer. No I won't go. Mama said I couldn't sing. She just said it once. Yet, I've carried her rejection all these years. What parents say to children is powerful. I can sing. I sing beautifully. My voice is beautiful. I'll train it by taking singing lessons. Mama please let me go!! I didn't go.

USE THE FOLLOWING LINES TO WRITE ONLY GOOD AND POSITIVE THINGS ABOUT YOURSELF-REGARDLESS OF PREVIOUS PARENTAL INPUT. FOCUS ONLY ON THE POSITIVE. USE AS LITTLE OR AS MUCH OF THE PAGE AS NEEDED.

For example: **I have skills, talents and creativity that are uniquely mine. I am worthy of all good things-especially sobriety!**

_____

_____

_____

_____

_____

_____

_____

_____

_____

_____

WHITE WHORE
11/16/94

     I attended a twelve step meeting today. I'm working on acceptance. In order to do this I ought to keep the focus on Queen today. It's so easy blaming circumstances outside of me for my perceived inadequacies. I am enough!

     Kelly called today. She was drunk as a dog. She's a piece of white trash, seeking salvation at the head of black dicks. She's a choosy whore though. Professional sports niggahs whet her appetite. She knows most are fucked up in the head. She thinks they'll supply her with unlimited "highs" and "niggah fucks" just because she's white. I hate to admit it- but she's right. Get that stupid niggah, white whore. Take all of his money. Just don't let the muthafucka knock you up. If you do, you're in the same boat as most black mothers- single, mad and broke. Ah, of all the pages in this book-this is probably one of the most controversial. **What do you think? Be candid and honest. Remember this book is designed to help you. We must face all of our fears,**

angers and resentments.

FOCUS ON QUEEN
11/17/94

Delores called today. She's nice. Delores is chairing our twelve step meeting today. Our meeting topics were:

Relationships
Sex (yummy)
Desire to stop drinking
Being human (another excuse for indiscriminate fucking and drinking)
Dealing with sobriety

Discussion meetings breathe life into my sometimes lethargic ass. I feel better after such meetings. I'm glad the only requirement is a desire to stop drinking. That's all I can digest today.

Today is a new beginning and I'm going to keep coming back. Recovery is a gift. It is a blessing. Why was I chosen, picked or should I say plucked out of the muck and mire of self-destruction and hatred? I've only just begun. Sometimes a really ignorant SOB will fall through the doors of recovery. Oh yeah, like I'm so brilliant. My beautiful ass wouldn't be here if that was the case. I mean who's kidding whom? I'm sitting in this chair because I thought I was so fucking smart and cool. Now I'm pleading for these SOB's to help me. What a truly humbling experience.

I was killing myself and these people were my last sanctuary of hope. How can I use my shitty past to help others? They suggest I don't shut the door on my past. Thank God for my ability to choose sobriety today. There is hope for me and my alcoholic mind.

Today I will remember my recovery is my responsibility. Repetition is the key to the mental revolution I am undergoing. Hearing the same thing over and again is foremost today. Is it really necessary to change Queen to meet the condition? What's the condition anyway? Frederick Douglass said agitate, agitate, agitate. For me agitate means tackling the defense mechanisms which led me to the bottle- fear, anger, resentment and slavery.

According to my idea of recovery, the more I attack the above, the better I'll live on a daily basis. My recovery program also suggests using steps, sponsors and ACCEPTANCE. Supposedly, ACCEPTANCE is the key to all my concerns. I'm maturing psychologically. This translates to "growing up" and letting go. That's letting go of people, situations and circumstance I cannot control.

Faith in my Higher Power is a must. There are so many things that I allow to make me feel guilty. I thought by binding my breasts during early adolescence, that my aunts would stop talking about me and my mama. There was so much whispering when I was around them. It never occurred to me they did the same thing. Where do I begin to wade through the ocean of lies and half-truths? Wade through my personal hellfire and brimstone. Why use sponsors! A sponsor is a teacher of sorts. They suggest strategies which have a proven success rate. I used sponsors more often than not during active alcoholism.

OTHER SPONSORS

Before I stopped drinking, I used sponsors. Some of my first sponsors or teachers were the people listed in the table below. Sponsors are guides. In twelve step programs, they share their experience, strength and hope with the newcomer.

* Mama: drunk and crazy
* Gilmore: drunk, woman beater, hated me
* Mr. Mack: my great aunt Ruth's lover, drunk, child molester

Lamar: Aunt Thelma's husband, woman beater, child molester, Napoleon complex
* Andrew: Thelma and Lamar's son, drunk, junkie, emotional abuser, child molester
* Uncle William: drunk, coward, emotional abuser
* Iceman: sugardaddy, heavy drinker, emotional abuser
* Alma: junkie, victim, my ghetto mentor
* James: Jamessa's father, drunk, Napoleon complex, guts
* Marvin: drunk, coward, woman beater
* Leonard: drunk, coward
* Charles: coward, friend, lover, mama's boy
* David: drunk, junkie, brother, rapist, thief, male / female abuser

So why in the fuck is it so strange and alien to accept help today? Why do I balk? Sobriety means recovery and life.

Why does this baffle me? You eagerly and readily accept all ideas, practices and suggestions from fools. So, why is it difficult to accept help from sober drunks? Oh you are so right. Grace sobered me up. There was a time in my life when I was willing to do anything for a drink-anything. I would also do anything for a tiny sliver of crack cocaine.

What about today? Am I willing to stay sober? My life is priceless. I will remember my life is so precious today. One day at a time, I will be free of self-centered fear. There are too many secrets. Will I ever reveal the secrets- all of them! **Use the following lines to write about your mentors.**

_____

_____

_____

_____

_____

_____

_____

_____

_____

_____

_____

_____

_____

_____

_____

_____

_____

_____

_____

_____

_____

MOLESTATIONS II
11/18/94

The childhood molestations were abhorrent. Lamar and Andrew were the worst of the child demons. The "others" were the drinking buddies of mama. She'd wake David and me at odd hours of the morning. The three of us would walk barefoot under the starry Alabama sky, to the foreboding haunts of the niggah drunks. Excuse me that's a shack of drunkards, my mother included. The shack was one large room. For example, most homes have a kitchen, living room, bedroom, bathroom, closet, and so forth. Not so in the shack. It was sectioned off by dirty sheets. The "bedroom" was separated from the rest of the "shack" by the sheet. The floor was made from long rectangular planks of wood. Dirt was under the planks. The outhouse was a few yards from the shack. The room was lit by the fireplace and kerosene lamps.

At times throughout the drinking, cussing, lying and card playing debauchery, this stinking, moldy man would appear seemingly out of nowhere and grope me. My brother and I were supposed to be asleep behind one of the "room dividers." Somewhere deep inside my young mind, I knew this was wrong. Yet, because of some strange quirk in my nature, I felt liable for his actions. How can a child be responsible for the actions of a grown, rusty, musty, smelly man? That's like a newborn baby giving birth to a full grown woman.

Children in abusive and alcoholic families believe they are the reason everything is so bad. They feel if they weren't born, everything would be right in the world. I believed my mother didn't love me. She would beat me mercilessly for the slightest infraction. Sometimes after a brutal whipping, I'd count my welts. Sometimes I would trace the patterns left by the three plaited switches, or ironing cord and straps.

Mama said malicious things to and about me. My

mother was a physically beautiful drunk. She ate very little and walked practically everywhere when we were in the south. Along with being a laundress, she was a beautician. What irony! My mother did everyone's hair but mine. She seemed to show preference for my younger brother and sister, David and Gloria.

You know what to do, so get busy! Spill the poison.

_____

_____

_____

_____

_____

_____

_____

_____

_____

_____

_____

_____

_____

_____

_____

_____

_____

_____

_____

_____

SISTER, SISTER
11/18/94

Gloria was my only sister. The mention of Gloria's name brings back painful memories. She was a sneaky little bitch. Mama woke me up when she went into labor that October night. It was 1961, I was seven years old. I just thought mama had a big stomach. She was single and our family looked upon her pregnancy as a disgrace. It didn't matter that other females in the family conceived out of wedlock. The difference was my mother didn't give a damn. Alcohol was her god. She cared not an iota for public opinion. Wilma did what she wanted, when she wanted and with whomever she wanted to do it with.

Afraid and sleepy, I went for help along snake infested dirt roads in Tuskegee. I was so jealous of Gloria. Along with David, my younger brother, I was also charged with Gloria's care. It was common in the south for young children to care for even younger siblings.

Years later, after mama's overdose, Gloria came to live with me in the projects. I opened the doors of my Parkside home to Gloria. She said she wanted to leave my Aunt Nell. I believed her. I took her in. I was betrayed. It hurt me so much. She was slated to graduate from Kiser High School in Dayton, Ohio. Arrangements were made for her to have a nice prom. I'd sold my ass to get the money for this prom. That fall of 1979, she was to attend Central State University, in Wilberforce, Ohio. I wanted a better life for my sister. I wanted more than what she gave me in later years. My sister hated me or did I hate her and disguised it. Whatever, in September, after graduation from Kiser High School, she left for Central State University. Then all hell broke loose.

On this October weekend Gloria was home and very depressed. It was then my sister shared that she'd missed four menstrual cycles. Gloria hadn't told the sperm donor anything. She was afraid and asked me to listen on the other phone while she talked to him. His name was Gary. He was one of the maintenance men who worked in Parkside

Homes. He wanted her only for sex. He had someone else in his life and after hearing about the pregnancy hung up. She cried. At the time, I was half drunk and in no mood for tears. "What are you going to do?" I scowled. At the time, Ohio didn't terminate a pregnancy after ten weeks.

One week after Gary (the sperm donor) hung up, Gloria, my young daughter and me were on our way to Detroit, Michigan for a five hundred dollar abortion. As we drove through the cold, dark night I wondered about many things. My tangerine orange Chevy Vega wasn't road worthy. There were starter, battery and ignition problems. Would my dilapidated Vega cut off on the highway? Who would help us? Would it restart after I turned the ignition off? I was half drunk throughout the duration of the trip. We did what was needed and returned to Parkside Homes. Shortly after the abortion, Gloria fled Ohio and moved to Seattle with a cousin.

Years after helping my sister with her abortion, she tried to help me. I didn't see it that way. During an August 1988 night, my daughter had enough of my indiscretion and licentiousness antics. She reached out for help and it was available to her. My daughter called her Aunt Gloria, who was visiting family in Cleveland at the time.

I had been taken to jail for target practice with the washing machine. My mind was viewing the help my daughter needed, as theft. I believed my relatives stole my daughter. My sister was the ring leader. Her accomplices were several of my mother's sisters. Those same sisters, who wouldn't take me in after mama's death, kidnapped my child. In my booze burned mind, this is what happened. The reality was they were protecting my child from a mean, brutal, hardhearted and incapacitated drunk. I hated them all, my sister included. My drunkenness was cited as the reason for the removal of my daughter. I could care less. The following day, I got drunk after being released from jail.

My soggy booze brain rationalized all of my actions. I said my aunts hated my independence. Along with my mama, they were raised to be dependent on my grandmother. Because of my mama's insanity and drunkenness, I was fiercely independent. I believed I never needed them or my daughter. That's another thing about alcoholism; the denial aspect is so strong. I couldn't see how weak and out of control I really was.

As a child and adult, I was jealous of Gloria, my sister. In childhood, I treated her the way mama treated me, cruel and with contempt. Mama loved Gloria and David. She didn't seem to love me one bit. Well, in recovery, acceptance is still the key. Prayer leads to acceptance. Can I change anything or anyone outside of myself? No, I can't. I was dead, now I'm alive. I was blind, now I see. Today, I'll pray for willingness. I must have willingness to accept what I can change and leave the rest alone. Who do I recognize as a winner? Right now, it's the rich and beautiful-that's it. Am I right? Am I? Is being rich and beautiful enough for me? What am I saying? Values and value systems ought to determine winners.

Are sober drunks winners? The bum who stinks and reeks of only twenty-four hours of sobriety-is this person a winner? The answer is yes, a resounding yes. Sobriety is built upon the concept of one day at a time. Once we cease to engage in limiting and self-defeating behavior, we become winners- IMMEDIATELY!! Disrespecting ourselves by drunkenness, obesity, poor hygiene, deceitfulness, etc., are all self-defeating behaviors. I know my belief system is in need of a major overhaul. An entire psychic change is in order. My childish ego has been allowed to run rampant far too long.

NEUROSIS BREAK

Today this man saw me in the shoe repair shop. He tried to give me his phone number. I'll not involve myself with active drunks and junkies, no matter how good I imagine the dick to be. I know him from times past. NO!   NO!   NO! **Use to congratulate yourself for working through a <u>neurosis break</u>.**

_____

_____

_____

_____

_____

_____

_____

_____

_____

_____

_____

_____

_____

_____

_____

_____

_____

_____

JOB HUNTING
11/21/94

It's the civic duty of every American to visit the capitol. I was in the capitol, Washington, D.C. and it was crazy. What a trip. I literally mean trip. Niggahs were everywhere. Doing nothing! Going down slow, going down fast! Slave minded niggahs all over the place.

I applied with the federal government while there. The position was Risk and Health Specialist. Although I wasn't hired, I'm truly blessed. I've endured and overcome much trauma. I've tackled enough trauma and betrayal to douse the brightest flames. I want to be a beautiful movie star. I am a glamorous, sexy, voluptuous goddess  of life. I want to meet a rich man, who'll snatch me out of the poverty zone. I'm going to love him where it feels good, and that's all over. He deserves the best. I am the best! I told you this was a neurosis break. I am still looking to be rescued. When will I have enough self confidence to realize I am enough? I am enough.

Use the lines below to describe yourself- as you are today.

_____

_____

_____

_____

_____

_____

AUNTIE RUTH
11/23/94

I'm in a twelve step meeting. Thoughts of freedom race through my mind. Someone saw "confused" written across my forehead and suggested I read the Celestine Prophecy and Egyptian Myths and Legends. I suggested they read all the works of Joel Augustus Rogers, Ben Jochannan, Ralph Ginzburg, Cheikh Anta Diop and John Hope Franklin-just get the fuck away from me!

The longing to touch and see her, went on for over a quarter of a century. Now because of Grace and sobriety, my dream had come true. I spent my first Thanksgiving in over twenty-five years with my great aunt, Auntie Ruth.

In the days of segregation, Auntie Ruth was a maid. She cooked, cleaned and generally slaved for Tuskegee's white upper crust. She did this almost sixty years. Aunt Ruth raised her own children and grandchildren during this time. In addition to that, she did the best she could for my drunken mama, her niece. I'd never known any aunt or loved any aunt the way I knew and loved Auntie Ruth. In many ways, she was dearer to me than Wilma.

Auntie Ruth was the "Great Lady" who frequently supplied my basic needs of food, clothing and shelter. She'd take white folks hand me downs, twice removed and repair them as needed. The discarded garments clothed the half-naked bodies of David and me. At the same time, Auntie Ruth would constantly chide mama about her constant boozing.

Auntie Ruth was one stabilizing force in mama's life during the Alabama years. Auntie Ruth took David and me under her wing. Again, because of mama's drinking, at age eleven, I was ripped from the care of this grand lady and sent to a foreign land- Cleveland, Ohio.

In the life of every drunk, there is at least one nurturing caregiver. Use the lines below to thank yours.

_____

_____

_____

_____

_____

_____

_____

_____

_____

_____

_____
_____
_____
_____
_____
_____
_____
_____
_____
_____
_____
_____
_____
_____

THE MAN
11/24/94

My mama and I were both pitiful. I think I loved her. I really don't know. Even to this day, I'm not sure. Mama was a drunkard and a sex slave when drinking. Her man was married. He was David and Gloria's father. I hated him and the feeling was mutual. Mama would go to any length for that man. It mattered little to her where they fucked. In front of David and me, in the same bed with us, there were no boundaries when she drank.

Was slavery the real culprit or was my mama just a slutty bitch? At least when I fucked, I sent my daughter to a babysitter or waited until I thought she was asleep. My daughter certainly has a story to tell. Jamessa, my daughter is sorely missed. I wish she loved me. Even so, it's time to move to another phase in recovery. I must be honest with me.

Some aspects of looking at the truth can be gory and ugly. However, we must confront our fears, angers and resentments. You know what to do.

_____
_____
_____
_____
_____
_____
_____
_____
_____
_____
_____

ANNETTE
11/27/94

The meetings help me. Today's topic was self-centered fear. Prayer removes fear in all of its grisly manifestations. At two o'clock today, Annette is supposed to start braiding my hair. Two o'clock could mean anytime from three o'clock on. Annette's the best hair braider in Dayton. Since I'm pretending to be flexible and tolerant, I'll be there at two o'clock. She too resides in a roach infested housing project.

It would be nice if she returned to high school. She only has a semester to go. One semester and only one-half credit to graduate. Why do people choose failure? So you think you're better than Annette-well, you're wrong. Hey hold it honey, why did you drink yourself silly for twenty plus years? You're not any better or less than anyone. My black wool coat goes to the cleaners today.

Take a minute or two and seriously point the finger at

someone. Just remember, three are pointing at you! Do it!

_____

_____

_____

_____

_____

_____

_____

_____

_____

_____

_____

STRATEGIES
11/29/94

The mental state of the child molester is lower than the lowest hell. It's time for another listen to Dante Alghieri's Divine Comedy. I'll design my motivational strategies so they'll attack the interests of a diverse audience. Inventory what's needed and salable. Spoiled emotional baggage has to be disposed of. Like spoiled fruit, it has to be thrown to the hogs. Today, Queen is throwing spoiled fruit to swine. In addition to that, what else must I let go of in order to be free? Why is it necessary to find the truth- especially the truth about me? The truth hurts.

Stinking thinking leads to drinking. That's what people say in the meetings. If it were true, every niggah and his mama would be drunk. Unfortunately, booze and dope only compounds our problems. I never intended for my daughter to become a street whore. It's a choice she made. She knows the difference between right and wrong. The consciousness I now possess is definitely anti-life. So where did it come from? Who's responsible? Is it right to trick and deceive myself? Not just sometime, but all of the time. Sobriety is the goal today.

List strategies you will use to attack drunkenness and remain sober today?

1._____

_____

2._____

_____

3._____

_____

4._____

_____

5._____

_____

REPETITION
12/3/94

I'm paying bills today. Pay my bills in a timely manner. This means on or before the due date. These damn bills never stop. What helps me in recovery is repetition. Repetition is the key. My goal today is to remain sober. Stay sober! Drink plenty of water. Pray for the removal of self-hatred and its many disguises. Pray for patience. Trust that my Higher Power will take care of me today. Pray for self-acceptance.

How will I design my business cards? Include:

Beautiful	Diverse speaker	Prescriptive exercise	State certified
Appointment X's	MS Ed	Color of card	What else?

How can I protect myself from cancer? Cancer killed my sister, Gloria. She was only thirty years young. Because Gloria waited until it was too late, by the time she saw a doctor, there was little if anything they could do for her.

My grandmother, Gussie also died of cancer. It was uterine cancer. Gussie, was ignorant and didn't believe in going to doctors, neither did my mother. Both mother and grandmother preferred "slave remedies" or folk medicine to modern medicine. My grandmother was at the point of no return when she sought medical attention for her illness. Take care of yourself Queen. I am so afraid of cancer. God help me with these fears. They seem to never go away. Exercise, eat healthy foods, pray and use the tools available in sobriety. Take care of yourself. Live, live-not just survive, live!

Graduate school was a farce and a cluster of stereotypical bullshit. I'll write my own book. I felt few, if any white professors cared about the educational vocation of black learners. I hold a Master's degree from one of the most prestigious institutions in Ohio, and I know less now than when I began graduate school. Frankly, I'm exhausted from the bullshit! Why would a thought about an anti-theft system for my automobile crop up at this time? More information is needed before I make a decision about this useless investment. If thieves want to steal my car they'll do so notwithstanding an alarm system.

THE FASHION SHOW
12/5/94

I attended a noon meeting today. The topics were:

11th step
Depression: causes, cures, ramifications

11th step Depression: causes, cures, ramifications Acceptance is purportedly the ability to live life on life's terms. Theoretically I'm to relate to the emotions, not compare situations. Well heck, that's asking a lot. Am I supposed to be a square peg, attempting to fit in a round hole? I model my behavior based upon what I've seen and allowed to creep into my consciousness.

I want a two million dollar a year business. In America, that isn't asking for much. When I was offered the job of fashion show commentator, I was ecstatic, yet apprehensive. After all, Margaret, the coordinator, was cunning and deceitful. Around 1986 or thereabouts, I'd fallen victim to her calculating schemes. Here's what happened- or I think happened? My memory was probably clouded by too much strong drink.

From 1986 to October 13, 1991, I was utterly entrenched in the throes of severe alcoholism. Booze and crack were my lovers. Everything, I mean everything-kids, bills, esteem etc, played second fiddle to these hydras. In 1986, I was working as a part time waitress at the golf course. Margaret was my boss. She watched me like a hawk. I would arrive at work half-drunk. I thought liquor didn't smell, but everyone knew I was smashed. I was the laughing stock of the golf course and viewed as a clown and a tramp.

In retrospect, I couldn't blame her. Years earlier, shortly after their arrival from California, in an alcohol induced haze I'd come on to her husband. Maybe it's because of her pity, that she tolerated me. Maybe it was because she understood addiction.

Several of Margaret's five daughters had fallen prey to the claws of alcoholism and addiction. After a while, Margaret tired of my antics and set me up. Maybe I set myself up. Whatever, she accused me of soliciting and fired me. I was pissed off. The ugly bitch! This I thought was her way of paying me back for fucking with her husband. Thank God, that's all that happened- a simple firing. I'd been fired before.

The fashion show was held at a local club. The proceeds went to a worthy cause- Margaret's purse. All clothes were local and many from the personal wardrobes of the participants. People from all walks of life attended and got into the act. White girls and their counterparts, mature, wrinkly white women whose greatest achievements occurred at the head of black dicks, were out in force. They vied for the attention of black brainwashed niggahs. The black girls with ADD disorder-All Designer Dresses knew their fates rested upon their minimum wage jobs, fake nails and fake straight hair styles.

The participant's bodies were all builds and sizes. You name it and that body type was in the show. Tracy is Margaret's youngest daughter. She's also the biggest, broadest and most awkward of her five sisters. She doesn't care for me. When I was selected as the show's commentator, Tracy gave me one of those phony no teeth smiles. In retrospect, it wasn't Tracy with attitude trouble, it was me.

I considered her a spoiled, ugly, funny-bodied bitch. I was jealous of her relationship with her mother. Tracy was a sneaky fuck-up and Margaret knew it. Tracy had the peculiar habit of selecting sorry, misfit men and for a time was snorting coke and smoking crack cocaine. Regardless of what happed in Tracy's life, Margaret always bailed that bitch out of trouble. Why didn't she let her sink or swim? I had to sink or swim when I found myself in freedom compromising predicaments? My mama wasn't available to bail me out of trouble. Yes, my pretense at liking Tracy just aggravated the facts- we despised each other. Even during unexpected meetings, we'd speak only because it was the courteous thing to do.

I'd always wanted a mama like Margaret. This hard working woman loved her children, dressed sharp, had great conversation and was in control of her life. She had lots of friends. Margaret was well liked by many people. She never drank. My mama was none of the above. Like her daughter, Wilma was a drunk. She had no friends, no money and except for Gilmore, her lover, was totally isolated from others.

Yes, I was the culprit. I will stop people pleasing when it comes to Tracy. I want to stay sober today and therefore, I must pray for her success and happiness. Sobriety demands I ask for others the things I want for myself. Damn it!

Describe the "perfect" mama.

_____

_____

_____

_____

_____

_____

_____

_____

_____

_____

_____

_____

_____

_____

UNCLE WILLIAM
7/24/94

What's the significance of my mother's drunken brother, William in my life? I was so afraid of him, drunk or otherwise. I didn't trust Uncle William. He was mean and when intoxicated bullied women. After our arrival in

Cleveland in 1966, we lived in the attic of a "real" house located at 6901 Hough Avenue.

My grandmother and my schizophrenic Aunt Marge lived on the first floor. Aunt Mercedes, her husband and seven children lived in the two bedrooms, one bath on the second floor. After a while, they purchased a house. It's was rumored my mother, Wilma, loaned Mercedes the down payment on that house. If she did, it was with her retirement money from Tuskegee's veterans' hospital. It was only a short time, before Uncle William and Aunt Delores moved to the now vacated second floor. I never wondered why we didn't relocate from the small attic to the roomier second floor.

The first thing Uncle William did when drunk, was aggravate my grandmother. For hours he would walk between the first and second floors cursing and verbally lashing out on the subject of past misdeeds in his life. He bellowed like an alligator while blaming my grandmother for all the wrongs in his life. One day, I was on my way downstairs to the first floor and heard him cursing as he walked up the steps to the second floor. Fear gripped me. We met between the flights He was terribly drunk. Should I rush past without speaking, should I say "excuse me," should I call out for help? I didn't know what to do. He reached for me! Right there on the step-he reached for me. It was a forbidden reach, it was taboo. He kissed my mouth. My young full, luscious lips were forced upon the drunken ones of my mother's brother. I felt faint. Would the New York scenes be repeated in this house? If I told, I knew no one would believe me. I would run away before I went through that again.

The door on the first floor was hurriedly opened. He let me go. I flew down the steps two at a time. Thoughts of rage, and madness at Uncle William, Lamar and Andrew raced through my stricken brain. Legs please move faster. In an instant, I was on the first floor. My grandmother was standing in the kitchen door, innocently calling him to dinner. At the time, my grandmother's Cleveland children, were in their thirties and forties. However, they responded to her in a manner similar to toddlers. Afraid to stop running down the steps, I zipped past my grandmother and went out the side door of the house.

My sanctuary was the tiny back porch. There was a vegetable garden and dog in the backyard. On the stoop, out in the open air, I felt safe. I don't recall how long I sat on the stoop. It really doesn't matter. For the time being, I was safe.

No one ever talked with me about puberty and its changes. It was as if the cloak of ignorance had permeated every nook and cranny in the consciousness of my supposed caregivers. At the time, to my way of thinking, men were to be feared, left alone and or killed instantly. Whenever I encountered men, it was always with a feeling of terror and forebode. Would the men beat rape or in some other manner assault me? Oh the horror of trying to decipher the madness. Would I ever love a man without fear or manipulation? When would I see men as kind, sensitive, compassionate and capable of love and tenderness? Would I ever see myself as worthy of the above from them? There are too many Black women who subconsciously chose whoredom as a way out of abusive relationships and homes.

This isn't the way, Puddin,' you don't have to sell your wares on street corners. Get your dumb ass off the street corner. Don't you realize you've been tricked-tricked big time? It hurts so badly.

You've sobered up. You receive word that your kid is a well-paid prostitute or some other menace to society. What will you do?

_____

_____

NANA AND BUTCH
7/24/94

     As a child, I frequented a playground a few blocks from 6901 Hough Avenue. The route I took required I pass1734 East 70th. This was the home of Nana and Butch. They were mother and daughter. Although I was piss poor, I was raised in the "southern" tradition of speaking to old people. When I was in the south, I was expected to speak to old people in both communities. This was a requirement of young and old alike. It was considered ill mannered to walk past an elderly person and not speak. I remember receiving a beating as a young child for not speaking to an elderly man on the way home from Booker T. Washington Elementary School in Tuskegee. He told my mama I hadn't spoken to him. What was ironic is that he was a bootlegger and mama was one of his regular customers. The decrepit, old, wicked, tattling son of a bootlegging bitch.

Therefore, when I'd walked past the home of Nana and Butch, I'd throw up my hand, smile and holler "good afternoon" or whatever. They responded in kind. This exchange went on for quite a while. From afar, I grew to love this elderly duo. Butch and Nana loved each other. They had a beautiful relationship. I longed for their kind of closeness with my mother.

Whether it was on television, radio or live, Nana loved baseball. In 1969, I had no patience for America's favorite pastime. It seemed boring and endless. Nana would sit, face cupped in her hands listening intensely to the radio or watching a televised game. The Cleveland Indians were her team. How could she sit and listen to a radio or watch television as though she were spellbound? Baseball literally hypnotized her. What I saw were grown men using a bat to knock a ball as far as they could. The men on the other team would attempt to catch the ball and throw it as far as they could before the batter made it to a base. Today, I enjoy this lazy game. It is very relaxing and helps my patience.

Butch loved crossword puzzles. On a daily basis, with her good left hand, she would painstakingly finish the Cleveland Plain Dealer's crossword puzzle. She was a stroke victim and dragged the right side of her body. It was a devastating stroke, which left her maimed physically, but stubborn and determined mentally. This half-woman performed all the so called normal functions of any other woman. Butch took care of her personal hygiene, clothed herself, washed and dried her clothes, bathed and took care of her dog, Teddy. She played the numbers and performed a host of other self-care chores. She loved herself and was a devout Catholic to her death. Butch was the best clinical psychologist I've ever known. She had but a high school education, yet she had a keen understanding of human motivation and behavior.

At age thirteen, I attempted suicide and would have been successful had God not intervened. I was now fourteen and experienced recurrent flashbacks from the near fatal drug overdose. I felt lonely, rejected and depressed. I reached out to these wonderful old people. Butch would tell me "I was one in a million." I believed her! Today, I know she was right. I enjoyed my visits with Nana and her daughter. Since they were elderly, I inquired as to whether they had any chores I could do around the house. Their home was beautiful, compared to the sparse, old-fashioned hand me down furniture my grandmother owned.

How Nana could cook! She made delicious grape wine. When it was available, I would sneak into the refrigerator after they'd become engrossed in the nightly television ritual and drink my fill. I replaced what I'd drink with water. They never questioned me about the watered down elixir.

NORMALCY?
7/25/94

What was normal during my childhood? Is self-hatred so deeply entrenched in my psyche? Oh boy! Here are just a few of the traumas I've lived through thus far in my short life.

Alcoholism	Racism
Low self-esteem	Hypocrisy
Beatings	Sexual abuse
Poverty	Suicide attempts
Hunger	Wanton emotional cruelty

In a sense, the above represents normalcy in quite a few households-especially poor, black households. Wilma, my birth mother, was superstitious to a fault. What a poor deluded woman, I feel remorse for her today. She was a looker, yet intellectually and psychologically scarred. She deeply internalized the plight of her sisters and brothers and was discerning to a fault. Wilma was a most beautiful femme fatale. Mama was tall, slender and built like a brick shithouse. I know nothing of her childhood. Was she happy, sad, raped, abused or treated with respect and dignity as a youngster? The answers to these questions, I will never know.

In the south during the 1920's and 1930's, negro children were harshly disciplined. In many families, animals fared better than black children. To this day, I debate what name I prefer. I am called "niggah" by blacks and "nigger" by others. Is Teresa or Queen to complicated? Am I truly the wretched of the earth?

It seemed to me that my mama lived to drink, fuck and run away from reality. Wilma was a tragic character that strode across the stage of life swathed with heavy chains. Her sad tale reminds me of the trickery committed against Ophelia. How Ophelia strived to please everyone. They all took advantage of her love for prince, Hamlet. Like my mother, Ophelia died tragically and was buried. Oh what despondent women! Wilma, I loved and hated you simultaneously.

What do you consider "normal?" Have you ever considered that "normal" is really a misnomer?

_____

_____

_____

_____

_____

_____

_____

_____

_____

_____

_____

_____

_____

_____

_____

_____

_____

_____

_____

_____

FRIENDS?
7/25/94

I've wondered why I care little for entertaining in my home. Here's the reason. As a child there was such confusion, violence and emptiness in that place called home. I lived like a wild, untamed beast. Many days, I survived by eating wild berries, birds and nuts. I would knock birds out of trees with my homemade sling shot. My great Aunt Ruth would fry my kill of usually three or four sparrows.

The secrets of Cleveland, Brooklyn and Tuskegee

permitted few if any friends. I remember playing with only a handful of children while attending P.S. Eleven in Brooklyn. There were no visits from other children to my Brooklyn hellhole. Lamar and his filthy son were too busy raping and abusing my body and soul to tolerate the possibility of their dirty little secret being told to other children.

The only children who visited our Tuskegee shack were the ones we fought with as children. Living on Hough was another matter. Hough was different. We had indoor plumbing, electricity, running water and a real gas stove. One or two childhood friends were welcomed. However, I made hardly any friends in Cleveland. I was afraid they would find out about my mother's drinking. I was afraid of the poverty in which I was enshrined.

There was Tanya S. and Diana S. Tanya and I knew poverty and want. Diana knew neither. Diana lived on the same street as Butch and Nana. Diana was scrawny, unsightly, spoiled and vindictive. She couldn't be trusted. She had a goofy cousin, called "Brother." I had a crush on him. He was a short boy with large, fleshy lips and a set of sparkling white teeth. Since I was accustomed to indigence and scarcity, Diana's home appeared splendid. It was well furnished and ultra modern. Her grandparents were bootleggers. In addition to that, her grandfather worked a traditional job. Diana's mother, like mine, was a helpless and hopeless drunk. When I visited, Diana's mama was either stone sober and melancholy or drunk and in someone's way. It didn't matter to me; I'd seen this erratic behavior too many times before. I simply ignored her. All I wanted was to go to Diana's room. She had the latest clothes, toys, gadgets, candies, wine and marijuana.

One day at a time, those days are over. It's a blessing watching my hand write down my thoughts. Thanks God for sobriety.

What childhood friend(s) did you consider as living a "charmed life?" What's a "charmed life?"

HATE
7/25/94

I hate Cleveland. I abhor my Aunts. I have ill feelings toward my brother. I despise my mama. I hate myself. I never knew my father, and I abhor him most of all. He left me unprotected and I suffer from insecurity to this day. I always wanted to be happy and accepted. Who or whom did I want to accept me? Why- everyone! I want absolute perfection. I want happiness and freedom. Is this possible in America? Why was I spiritually dead during my most bountiful years?

Even today, I feel as though I don't fit anywhere. It's a "psyche" game and I'm the fall gal. When Amos N. Wilson writes about me, it hurts. There's no way I'm so thoroughly brainwashed.

Well that's how I was feeling on July 25, 1994. This is about staying sober no matter what! OK it's your turn. Hate is not an ugly word. It's one we are taught to feel guilty and ashamed about. Use it liberally below.

_____

_____

_____

_____

_____

_____

_____

_____

_____

_____

_____

_____

_____

GWEN W.
7/30/94

Gwen W. and I were drunk when we met. We frequented the same bootleg joints. I loved the underworld of bootleggers, boosters, pimps, whores, sugar daddies and the like. I was lost in my world of booze and drugs. I thought I was a star in the ghetto. Then as now, I craved attention and did what it took to get it.

Gwen was a little woman. She wanted to be large and strong. I am very tall and statuesque. I'm one hundred and eighty pounds of real woman. She's five feet one and ninety-five pounds of guts and gall. Gwen is brave and ready for action. For years, I believed I was a coward because of my stringent religious roots. Yet, under the influence of alcohol, I jeopardized my life and the lives of those whose company I frequented. The false courage alcohol gave me was so elusive. The fact of the matter is alcoholism is synonymous with cowardice. Thank God I am sober today.

In the ghetto, fighting is held in high regard. The same goes for fucking, pimping, stealing-everything but schooling. All the negative antisocial forms of group behavior are prized in the ghetto. Afterall, from birth onward we've been programmed to destroy self- destruct and loathe ourselves. Yes, this is going to be a great book. Gwen is sober today. Now where the hell did those thoughts come from?

Alcoholism is a one hundred percent irrational ailment. There is no way a real alcoholic can justify using it. That's what I mean-Alcoholism is a sick, sick, ailment. There is nothing cute or pretty about it. Use these words and explain the joy of your alcoholism and addiction. *You're on top of it, Dynamite, Beautiful Work, Hip, Hip Hurray, Great Performance, You Brighten My Day, Remember, Love.* **It's dangerous**.

LIVE
7/31/94

I want to live. Yet I'm afraid to live and afraid to die. God please help me. I want to live. I am tired of being a brainwashed human-a niggah, a niggah, a muthafuckin' niggah! In five days, I'll graduate with a Master's degree. A Master's from the whitest university this side of Ohio. The University of Dayton is seeped in conservatism, hypocrisy and money. Quite frankly, I will miss this demon in whiteface. I had many good days at the university.

Who will I invite to the graduation fiasco? I'll invite Annette, my hairdresser, and her family, Aunt Lillie, Tanya, Charles, the Cleveland family. Yes, they need to see me accept this degree. The black sheep of the family has done something worthwhile. The former black-out drunk has earned a Master's degree. The drunk who once believed salvation rested in the pennies of welfare and the bed of a housing project. This correspondence is possible through the generous contributions of a God of my understanding. Thank you, thank you. I'll do it one day at a time. Just one day at a time. Everyone I invited came to my graduation. What the hell is going on here?

Write a short and long range goal for yourself. Include your timelines?

_____
_____
_____
_____
_____
_____
_____
_____
_____
_____

SHOPPING
7/31/94

Mr. Cummings! Mr. Cummings was my dear, sweet, married lover. He was also thirty-two years my senior. What a kindly, dirty old man- a true blessing in disguise. It's time to go shopping. For a girl on welfare, with a fetish for booze and incompetent at child rearing, Mr. Cummings was my Prince Charming. He also took advantage of my ignorance of the financial world. This man had ghetto fabulous dollars. He never volunteered to invest money in my daughter's education, real estate, commodities or anything other than keeping me stone drunk and high. My protestations were kept to a minimum, if uttered at all. My thoughts centered on how I was *feeling*. Feelings not reason and rationalization controlled my every step. Today is the day I am satisfying my ghetto urge for shopping. Remember, the mind of the alcoholic is childish, self-centered and immature. Below is more proof of this fact.

Shopping List

Three dresses: Black,Gold, Red	Mascara: Maybelline	Perfume: California, Vanilla Musk
Make-up: Flori Roberts-pencils, powder, lipsticks	Juice: Apple, Orange, Prune	Cinnabar, Youth Dew and White Linen
Shoes: Match dresses	Fruit: Fresh apples	Panty hose: Hanes (six pair)

CHARLES' SISTER
7/31/94

I decided on an out of town meeting today. Yellow Springs, Ohio is forty miles east of Dayton. I craved the serenity inherent in a country ride. The lead speaker was a beautiful black woman. She was well groomed from head to toe. Since she was thin, and glamorous, I listened intently. This woman spoke of being reared in a dogmatic home headed by a mother drowning in the auspices of a hellfire and brimstone religion.

The lady spoke of several brothers and sisters in the family who were cursed with the disease of alcoholism and how it affected their household. Then she shared the location of her mother's current home and I was shocked. It was at this juncture, that I realized she was the sister of my then lover, confidant and puppet. I was unsure of what to call my man, so I referred to him as a spineless faggot. He has no balls whatsoever; a mama's boy in the truest sense. Well, after her talk, I decided to meet this woman.

I carry the malady of people pleasing and our initial meeting was strained. After introducing myself and making feeble attempts at establishing rapport, I was struck by a beam of awareness. Why was this female so callous and cold? I had never knowingly harmed her. The quiet voice inside me whispered "turn around" and then I knew. The man who accompanied her to the meeting had fixed his gaze upon me. I understood at once that the gory head of malevolence had once again shaken its angry locks. It was time to distance myself from venom. Why do I insist on people liking me? Is it absolutely necessary I dig everyone and visa versa? **This has to stop! HOW?**

_____

_____

_____

_____

DOLLS AND BREASTS
8/1/94

I met Pebbles through her sister, Annette. Her real name is Demetrius, but we call her 'Pebbles'. What a strange name for a chick. I think of the Flintstones everytime I hear it. As a child in Tuskegee, I recollect when the "Pebbles" doll was the rage. Mama bought me one. I loathed that doll. She had a bone in her hair. I guess the "bone" was what we today call a barrette. Whatever, I tore that doll to bits.
Yes the Barbie doll was for me. She had long, blonde, pretty

hair. I long for that hair even to this day. Barbie had a big chest, tiny waist and slim hips. Yes the perfect woman, albeit a white one. Due to my level of brainwashing, it didn't matter. Every negro girl wanted a Barbie doll with blonde hair and Shirley Temple curls. Nevertheless, let's return to this "tittie-breast" issue.

Pebbles has melon sized breasts. Her breasts nearly equaled the size of cantaloupes. She is physically ugly and toothless. But she has a beautiful set of breasts and five kids to match. Her breasts hang, shake and vibrate of their own accord. I've never seen her in a bra.

Beautiful breasts just mesmerize me to no end. I wish I had such. After the childhood molestations, childhood beatings and years of watching women brutalized, I ventured into adolescence uninformed and terrified of 'nature's way'. When my breasts started to develop I hid them under girdles. I wore the girdle because of the betrayal and invasion of my body by trusted family members. I thought of my uncle, Lamar and his son, Andrew, the Alabama drunks and babysitters who tarnished me mentally and physically. In my mind, men were strong and powerful and I wanted to be one. I wanted to be a man so I could fight off the invaders and body snatchers sure to appear in my future. At the time, I saw a woman's body being either ill-treated or suckling babies. I was so confused.

When my menstrual cycle started, I became paralyzed by psychological cramps. During the next three and a half years, the intensity of these cramps necessitated a monthly visit to the emergency ward. That's when the girdle was discovered. I didn't remove it until a classmate made fun of my flat chest in the ninth grade. When my mother and grandmother died, so did the cramps. I want a Barbie doll figure.

These pages are the first time I've inscribed this

amount of ink in addressing such a serious issue. When I was first molested and brutally raped, I was barely seven years of age. At age seven, I didn't have breasts. Some where in the darkness of my underdeveloped psyche, I wanted to remain a "girl"- forever. If grown men would abuse me without breasts, what would they do to me with them? I was filled with anxiety. The women in my family acted as though breasts were offensive and sinful, always hiding them, yet deeply wishing to show them off. The women in my family were confused, afraid, ashamed and demented. The teachings of my grandmother warped their "fragile" minds.

I followed right in step. They prized legs and hips. Although subconsciously, I knew the body was one integrated unit- to my aunts, it was fragmented. I too engaged in viewing my body as fragmented. Thank God for taking care of my beautiful breasts. The girdle did minimal damage.

ONE EYED MAN
8/1/94

On February 19, 1992 my only sister, Gloria, died of cancer. She was thirty years young. Months before her death, I was working through the sibling madness. This cleansing process involved attending many twelve step meetings, exercise, proper nutrition and prayer-plenty of prayer.

One-eyed Ronald heard my infuriated words at a discussion meeting. Twenty years earlier he'd lost his eye in a drunken driving accident. One Wednesday, after a speaker meeting he approached me. Ronald talked as if he was genuinely aware of my sticky situation. He told of the rift in his family. To my way of thinking, that brief conversation was the end of it.

Exercise is a huge part of my rebirth process. More often than not, I jog, walk or cycle an eight point two mile stretch of bike trail that snakes around metropolitan Dayton. One afternoon, I was walking the bike trail and spied two men standing on the river bank. My intuitive self signaled "danger." However, upon closer inspection, I realized one of the gentlemen was Ronald. He is a short, stout, tan skinned man. At the time, he was broke, scruffy and freshly sober. Here I am, walnut brown, well nourished, tight assed and walking on the bikeway. Thank God, he knew me. I waved to them and he decided to join me. In my gut I knew any other woman would have had trouble in this tight spot. This was a man who'd raped women and fought large dogs with his bare hands.

We talked of families, niggahs, booze, dope and hosts of other "keep your mind off of my ass" subjects. It took four plus miles of serious walking, but I prevailed. That was years ago. As of this revision, September 21, 2002, Ronald is still sober and happily fucking whomever will oblige him. My interpretation of life is flawed. Now that I know and believe my version of life is faulty, what do I do? I'll continue to pray and journal my way to serenity, fun and happiness. Journaling is power. YUCK!

My enjoyment of sex was hampered because of the abuse and molestations suffered at the hands of loved ones and others. Write how you were scarred by the sickness of a family member or trusted family friend. As awful as it may sound, these people are sick and in order for us to heal, we must become willing to forgive them.

_____

_____

_____

_____

_____

_____

_____

_____

_____

_____

_____

_____

_____

_____

_____

_____

_____

_____

_____

_____

_____

ILLEGITIMACY
8/1/94

My mama taught me it was a sin to bear illegitimate children. She bore three bastard children. My grandmother, Gussie Lee was ill at ease with us. Grandmother was purportedly pregnant when she married my grandfather, Yancy. I loved my grandfather. He wanted desperately to save my mother from the perils of alcoholism.

One of the causes of Wilma's depression was her subconscious guilt at bearing three beautiful bastard children. She felt she'd failed and disgraced the family name. What damn family name? We were all niggahs, poor black ass niggahs, in the white man's south. The south built a multi-billion dollar economy on the backs of illegitimate black babies.

Throughout the Parkside decade and half, I met many people. I hadn't seen any of my old Parkside buddies in years.

Today, I ran across Carrie J. Here's our story. For twelve of those fifteen plus years, I resided at 1208 Lima Place. Emma, Carrie's mother, lived two doors over in the same building. So why did I consider myself better than Carrie? Was it because I had one bastard compared to her five? I was blind and could see only "sin."

I painted a defective image of an alcoholic's life-my life. Moving into Parkside represented a dream deferred. Alcohol, teen pregnancy and motherhood were all I knew. My acting/entertainment career had to be put on hold, seemingly forever. You see, I actually believed I'd be discovered. This is how I pictured my "discovery." I'm walking down the street and a limo would pull alongside and whisk me into a world of glamour, money and stardom. I'd pretend I was Marilyn Monroe. Dorothy Dandridge, Diane Carroll, Lena Horne, and Eartha Kitt weren't good enough. Plus, I never saw them in the glamorous, sex kitten roles which turned Marilyn into a world wide icon. Marilyn was beautiful. She was a prized, neurotic white whore with a black woman's body. Her place among the stars was guaranteed. It's time to move on. I'm beginning to ramble.

Whom do you admire? Why?

_____

_____

_____

_____

_____

_____

_____

_____

_____

_____

_____

_____

_____

_____

_____

_____

_____

_____

_____

_____

_____

_____

_____

_____

?'s & EXCUSES
8/4/94

Today is my graduation day. The University of Dayton has one of the strangest looking university president's I've yet to see. In his commencement discourse he shared the usual senseless patronizing idioms, which the well-to-do take for granted. The cards are stacked in their favor. The education game becomes more sophisticated and deadly, the closer a drunk gets to the doctorate. The doctorate is the ultimate fuck in education. Ghetto alcoholics have to devise new success strategies. That's enough ink on my graduation.

My heart and head are becoming symbiotic and holistic or is it wholistic. This is not a good time for etymology. Society teaches the separation of heart and head. We are taught to fragment our personalities. This effort at fragmentation is futile; and for the alcoholic it's impossible. Alcoholics always lead with emotion. It is emotion that produces alcoholism. A drunk's heart and head are synchronized. Furthermore, most drunks live in the past, have a shitty value system and will flounder at the gates of Dantes Inferno before changing their wretched mindset. This brings me to my FISEPS model. FISEPS is an acronym for financial, intellectual, social, emotional, physical and spiritual values. I'm acted upon by a vast number of ideals, ideas and ideologies.

When will I learn to look at life as a semi-permeable membrane? It's not set in stone. My prehistoric opinions on the subjects of success, wealth, happiness, love and sex, are slowly killing me. Am I using the unwaveringly constants of race and gender to justify my muddled thinking? Am I using a poverty-stricken philosophy to authenticate sloth?

Sobriety is teaching me to handle such distortions. Today, sobriety is first and foremost. I place great emphasis and weight on the financial "F" in the model. Check this out, I never disciplined myself to invest and save money. I spend it as fast as I can get my hands on it. Go figure. I'll ditch this topic for a later attack.

Intellectual acuteness is imperative. It's very important. As a young child, I was rather bright during elementary school. This was my way of excelling and reaping praise from my caregivers. I was like a rolling stone and passed around from relative to relative, so I was constantly acting and smiling. Wilma never praised me. Gussie Lee didn't either. Maybe they weren't praised. One cannot give what they don't have. Living and loving is so historical and cyclic.

Learning to think in a logical, coherent, and rational manner is difficult for me. Subconsciously and consciously this is usually a chore. It's a chore because like Skinner's rats, I'm accustomed to others controlling my environment. Controlling my own environment, money and life, ought to be paramount. During drunkenness, I felt I was in control of "me." It too was a tremendous investment in "nothingness."

The pseudo belief that I was in absolute control, while at the mercy of others was ludicrous. So many times, I stumbled out of Dayton's Swat's Club howling like a wolf or barking like other rabid canines. Many times, I entered and exited bootleg joints blind drunk. It makes my jaws tight thinking about it. So many times, I placed myself in the clutches of evil, disguised as beauty. There were many days and nights I ventured into the valley of death and emerged safe and sound. But for the Grace of God.

I know there is a God. I sometimes feel the presence of God. I am learning to accept God's mercy and protection. I invested every moral fiber in anti-life dealings, so why not trust my Higher Power today. My lack of confidence was hidden under my beauty and degrees. My lack of confidence was hidden behind my wardrobe, car, job and bank account. My lack of confidence was hidden behind the men I chose for companions. Yes, Teresa Queen Johnson, let the poison flow. It's time to heal. Heal Yourself! You have the answers. You have always had the answers. Use them.

Use selective solitude, frequent meditation and constant prayer. Alcoholism promotes isolation and loneliness so we will use solitude on an infrequent basis. Therefore, we will have no confusion between therapeutic solitude and intentional isolation. I am becoming a social woman. We enjoy people. We will use prayer and meditation on a daily basis- every civilization uses it. Yes, Teresa Q. God loves you- always have and always will.

What's making a difference today? Why even attempt to make a fucking difference? Systematically and methodically alcoholics have taught themselves to live in an anti-life manner. I've been beaten, raped, neglected, half-starved and mocked. Why should I even dare to **"think"** I can make a difference? That's another thing- why even **think?** Alcohol and dope appeared to make it easy to forget. So abstinence is revolutionary. To not pick up a drink today, represents a revolutionary gesture.

Who said alcohol is the elixir of the gods? In my hands it's a lethal weapon. It's already cost me my job, man, sanity, self-respect and my daughter. Why would I choose to return to something I know I cannot handle. It's because of the conditioning. It's a "Skinnerian" pattern that runs so deep. I'll never entirely uproot its influence in my life. Higher Power, who resides within this flesh-please keep me sober today. Please! Please! Please! I know and have known for sometime, that I'm suicidal. Why am I suicidal? Is it because I'm weak and afraid? I've been subconsciously taught to destroy myself.

This disease wants me to destroy myself, by any means necessary. It's the conditioning. That's why I "cringe" when I spend money with people who look like me. I've been taught to hate myself. I've been taught to fear the changes central to successful living.

SOBRIETY MEANS THE FREEDOM
TO APPRECIATE MY FIVE SENSES
AND THE BEAUTIFUL WAYS THEY
ADJUST TO MY WORLD.

Yet, here's Queen committing a revolutionary gesture- a revolutionary act-just because I stay sober one day at a time. WOW! That's how I make a difference today. Staying sober represents freedom to redefine myself, freedom to gain an in depth understanding of external politics, freedom to appreciate my five senses and the beautiful ways they help me relate to the world.

Everywhere alcoholics go they impair, demolish and sever the truth. I thought I became a drunk because of familial concerns. Boy was I wrong and miseducated. I was taught alcoholism. I was taught to kill myself and cop out of life. I was taught to escape life and its bittersweet kisses.

God I need you more today than ever.

Live and Let Live!

You are opening my eyes with the spittle of Auser (Isis); please keep me sober throughout my enlightenment. Please keep me sober. Is slavery an excuse for nearly destroying myself with booze and dope? No it isn't! One of the gifts of sobriety is retrospection and introspection. Retrospection because I need to know my history. Introspection because I need to know how that history affects me today. Knowledge of history creates a sense of excitement, irritability and discontent within my present "psyche" and soul's evolution.

Knowledge of my history serves to enlighten me to the forces of destruction and their many disguises. In my life, alcohol is a destructive force. You see, I've accepted that a savage and beastly creature dwells in me. The aim of this creation is to kill, maim, and murder this drunk. Grace subdues this filthy horror within my soul. My indoctrination in European philosophy has been swift thorough and programmatic. All during my lonely life, I've been taught nothing but "white ideas."

Alcohol makes me feel powerful. Why shouldn't it? A poor, abused and neglected creature. Since I don't know who I am, anything outside of myself makes me feel powerful. Anything!! I never developed a sense of personal excellence in me. It never occurred to me that by virtue of being human-I am godlike.

Oh no, I don't want to talk about the chicken coup. Even today, the brutality still touches every fiber of my being.

My very existence and the existence of my family are because of the "chicken coup" and other ghastly acts. My slave great, great grandmother was hurt by this incident. It caused her resentment, pain anger and denial.

Her self-hatred coupled with an intense ability to survive, is the reason for my presence today. She beat the hell out of her children. Her man, my great, great, grandfather was lynched- death at the hands of parties unknown. These acts were committed by pathogenic and psychopathic whites.

Help me God! I need you more today than ever. I need your love, care and protection.

It's time I let go of "slavery" excuses!
It's time I let go of excuses to drink, drug and destroy myself!
My country needs my skills, talents and contributions!!
I need my skills, talents and contributions!

HAIRY, SCARRY
8/7/94

Oh boy! I feel as though I'm flipping out, going over the deep end. I've saved thousands of dollars. Oops, let me clarify that- I have access to a line of credit. I'm getting out of debt. My hands are burning, I must spend the money! Spend it! Spend it, my mind screams, spend it now!!! Yes, the psychologists are correct. Since I still possess a poverty mentality, I spend money as soon as I get it. Why? It's the fucking low self-esteem. I deeply believe things outside of me, make me. Exoteric rather than esoteric desires. One day at a time, with the help of my Higher Power I'm becoming conscious of the tricks. Poverty and alcoholism play mental tricks on my mind.

Here's comes another neurotic moment. I thought I was free of the hair obsession because I wore braids. I've changed my hair to every color of the rainbow. I've been bounced, wrapped, weaved, braided and microoed to no end. I must tell you about the "burn." My braids were beautiful. They were human hair, straight and long- oh so long and soft. I love long hair. I wonder why? So be it.

My natural, nappy hair thrives in braids. It was full, strong, elastic and dandruff free. The gorgeous hair of my ancestors extended well beyond my shoulders without the chemicals. These facts only whet my appetite for chemicals. I had this fabulous head of virgin hair and all I could think of was a perm. Had I once again lost my mind? This is such a sick and sad story, so prepare to burst your guts with laughter. With the beautiful mane I wore, I should have sought the best black hair professionals in the business.

Not me- that would have been too simple. I ventured into the halls of the unlearned. I entrusted my mane to the unschooled and unskilled students of cosmetology. These students had not earned their licenses. Their teachers were barely feeding themselves and paying their own bills.

My initial greeting by an aloof high schooler should have tipped me off. "You here for Monet?" "What you want today?" I wanted to say 'Ms. Manners,' but sanity once again returned. What good would it do? I told her what I wanted. "Hold on" said the receptionist as she glanced impassively at me while continuing her phone conversation. After a lapse of thirty or more seconds, she quipped "that'll be eighteen dollars." For what? "Overlays" was the reply. "I'm not here for overlays today." "Oh ok, what you want done?" "I want a relaxer today." "What kind do you want," she asked. "I don't know its virgin hair." "Who do you want to do it?" "Someone who's good," I said. "Well, Michelle is good," was her reply. "Ok" was mine.

After five minutes of standing and listening to "nothing," I was finally offered a seat. Actually, I was being obstinate and checking whether they were on their toes and offered customers a chair. They failed in that department. It wasn't long before Michelle appeared. We talked briefly. With no suggestions from her supervisor, Michelle decided on a very popular relaxer. Throughout preparation of the hair product, the state certified teacher never stopped to confer with either patron or student. I also said nothing.

"Ouch my scalp is burning!" "I'm getting ready to wash," she said as she lowered my chair, and we walked to the basin. As she rinsed, rinsed and rinsed, thoughts of "bone straight" hair ran through my mind. In my imagination I was speeding in a drop top, black Allante. My lover was coffee bean brown, with biceps of steel. He was wearing a white ripped "T" shirt and denim shorts, which exposed massive sable thighs and legs. Yum! Yum! My shorts were white and torn in all the right spots, showing my exposed navel. I was wearing a navy blue polka dot bustier. My make-up consisted of lipstick, brown liner and mascara. My long, straight tresses were blowing in the wind. Whipping all over my face and smelling so good. My jet black hair which was shiny, soft and long- just like the white girls.

Suddenly, the vision vanished. I was startled when Michelle said "Miss Ann, come here." I knew something was wrong, but first I needed to know whether my hair was straight. Well let me tell you, not only was the hair straight, it was gone! My hair was in the sink, on the sides of the sink, in her hands-everywhere but on my head. I was aghast! I was stunned!!! I was bald!"

**ONE DRINK IS TOO MANY
AND A THOUSAND ARE NOT ENOUGH!**

Miss Ann, Miss Ann, come here," yelled Michelle. Michelle was an unlicensed student.

I had entrusted my beautiful mane to a student. Because I wanted to impress the school personnel, I lost my mane. Saving a few bucks was the first part of this trilogy. The second was I thought the people in the school were my friends. Lastly, I was trying to impress this supervisor who lived to take diet pills. My figure was so beautiful and taunt. This supervisor watched me constantly.

How had pseudo vanity and low-self esteem caught up with me? Once again, I put the perceived needs of others above my own. Once again, I was stung. You see, now I was bald-headed and sober. I was still a drunk, although sober, still a bald-headed insecure drunk. This means I'm still whitewashed.

BIG TIME
8/7/94

I rented a $450.00 limo for graduation. I must salute the poverty complex, it's a subtle whore. I had to play the 'big shot."

I could've given my ex-sister in-law, Renee, and the kids cash money for shoes and clothes. They needed both. What the fuck, they don't appreciate me. I'm always bending over backwards to help people. I do it because I've been taught it's the right thing to do. I do it because I want to be liked and appreciated. I do it because it makes me feel I'm contributing to a divine cause; or do I? It's what the "old" folks taught me. The less fortunate are reminders that poverty is just around the bend. Who's going to help me? What about me being less fortunate? Those people, (Renee and family), never call and say "hello," "how are you today?"

Renee is lazy and ignorant. She lies around the house. Food has become her God. The children are out of control. Hold it, check in time. Whom do you call yourself talking about? For the record, your daughter, Jamessa is a prostitute-a low-life street walking prostitute. She had a pimp's baby. Your granddaughter, Jasmine Charlene, was fathered by a pimp. This is the pimp who brutalizes your daughter. This pimp is on drugs. This pimp takes whore money and turns it into drugs. This low-life pimp, like your father, does not feed his children. How dare you ever say anything negative about anyone's child, when the mote in your eye is as large as a trash can. Your best bet is to pray for everyone involved in this scenario. Pray for their health, wealth and peace of mind.

I pray for those things. Yes, well pray harder and more often. God is all powerful in this. God is overseeing this whole series of events. Keep the focus on Queen! It's going to work out. Ridding the mind of defects requires action. In order to become happy, I must be willing to become honest. This means purposeful reading. Reading that's done to clear my mind of all misconceptions and misinterpretations, which were and are subconsciously hindering me.

For instance, whites are smarter. Big breasts are the key to a man's happiness. Long straight hair is the prettiest hair. Having lots of money is evil. Loving more than one man is amoral. What excuse are you making today? This losing weight obsession has to be dealt with. Let's go. I'm five feet ten inches tall. I weigh a solid 185lbs. I exercise religiously. Question- why am I concerned about losing more weight?

-SOBRIETY IS MY JOB TODAY!-

Sometimes I'm such a coward. I feel being big keeps men from hurting me. It probably goes back to the molestations in Brooklyn and Alabama. Then to, so many big, fat, black women are just plain unhappy and chronically depressed. All we have are our children. So many of our men are strung out, drunks, jailed or faggots. We've had to be mamas and papas to our children. The fat is an insulator. The food is the "lover" "husband" and "father" we never had, yet continuously crave. Slavery is still kicking our black asses. If the Jews remember the holocaust, why can't black people remember and study the effects of slavery in our daily existence? It's difficult to sweep booze, dope and teen pregnancy under the rug. It's out front for the entire world to see. The easier, softer way isn't to avoid conflict. The easier, softer way is to refrain from drinking today. When I refrain from drinking on a daily basis, my life is easier and more fulfilling.

-I AM RESPONSIBLE FOR MY ACTIONS!-

BITCH MILDRED
8/14/94

Family matters are a constant challenge in my life. That evil, lowdown, Mildred bitch. Where did she get the fucking guts to do what she did? She had the audacity to send me a graduation card and twenty-five lousy fucking dollars. I hate that fat, black bitch with a passion. If she were to die today, I wouldn't attend anything that reminds me of her memory. To top it all off, God has blessed that bitch in her evil.

Here's her story. I was going on twelve years old when we arrived in Cleveland. Aunt Mildred loved me at age twelve. At the time, I also liked her. Yet, I had no understanding of the deep love connections between my aunts, uncles or my grandmother and her children. At the time, I considered my aunts ignorant about sexual matters and afraid of their womanhood. Today, I realize this trait had been inadvertently passed down to me. I guess my aunts love me.

Mildred met and fell in love with Oliver. Now Oliver

was and remains a nice man. Yet this bitch provoked him constantly. Like my grandmother, this female wasn't satisfied unless she was hurting. Her efforts were well rewarded. Oliver blackened eyes and generally kicked serious Mildred ass. She was interfering and jealous of certain sisters. I liked her still.

Although younger than mama, she was the "boss"-one of Gussie Lee's (my grandmother) favorites. My mama followed her directives to the letter. Mildred was domineering from the start. She worked hard and with resolve saved money and soon began to acquire property. Now she is financially well off. Maybe I'll marry Oliver, her estranged husband, and take everything she owns. She stole my daughter. I want revenge.

I wonder whether this inability to form lasting relationships is related to being distrustful of commitment in practically any form. After mama's overdose, in the spring of 1971, I would no longer deal with my aunts. I was not going to tolerate their dominance, sexual perversion and closed minds any longer. So they left me alone. I was sent to a rather decent foster home.

I guess that's why mama or the aunts never told me about menstruation. Those females stifled my psychological growth and development. My period just happened. My vagina was feeling wet and mushy one day. When I wiped myself, I looked at a washrag covered with blood. I panicked. I thought something was wrong. It was only nature taking its course. Teresa was growing into a beautiful young lady. Oh, I'm getting away from that bitch.

The Mildred bitch is cunning. Since she is unhappy, she wants those around her unhappy. This is her unconscious motivator. This is the entire family's unconscious motivation. Then too, maybe I'm resentful of her power over the rest of the family. Keep the focus on Queen.

That's what I'm supposed to do. If I were Gloria, that night, would I have done the same thing? That answer is "yes."

I WILL SAY "YES" TO LIFE TODAY.

From whom did you learn about your reproductive system?

_____

_____

_____

_____

_____

_____

_____

_____

_____

SHOOTING SPREE
8/14/94

Let's review the events of August 28, 1989. What happened? I was on a drinking and drugging spree. Scavenger human beings that are attracted to the scent of booze, vomit and crack cocaine were in and out of my tiny Parkside apartment. There were people I'd never seen before. They were people I feared. My daughter was home. I sent her upstairs. This usually happened when I was drinking and drugging if she were home. These, "strange men," wanted to get "high." They were newly initiated crackheads. This made them extremely dangerous. Word had gotten around that I had money, gave away big dope and kept lots of booze. Therefore, a great many leeches became my "fast" friends.

All of the attention, all of the 'ghetto recognition," it was for me. I was a "star" in this living hell. This particular night, I was in rare form. I was drunk and totally out of control. I was also fearful of the strangers I'd allowed in my home. What could I do? The first thought which entered my mind was "shoot the pistol." Like any red-blooded American, I loved guns. I loved the way they frightened people. This is what I wanted to do to the strangers in my home-frighten them away. I wanted them to leave us in peace.

At the time, I was a pistol packing mama. I kept my 357 magnum or 38 special in a huge green purse. On this night to remember, it was in the living room. I retrieved the gun and fired a shot into the washing machine, which was located in the kitchen.

-"I WAS DRUNK AND TOTALLY OUT OF CONTROL"-

It never crossed my mind to just ask those men to leave. Now, here's the real truth. I was drunk. I was blind drunk and paranoid. I was blind drunk, paranoid and afraid. The false courage alcohol provided was just that, "false courage." At thirty-five years of age I'm afraid to live or die.

What a quandary. Alcohol was my trusted mistress. Without it I was restless, irritable, discontent and suicidal. With it, I was a raving barbarian. The problem was and always will be Queen. Why was I so unhappy? Why don't I have the guts to just blow my brains out? This is how I see the situation today. My mind is still suffering from the childhood effects of a lack of support in critical life areas.

Somehow, the subconscious desire for punishment and authoritarian rule is still with me. This feeling of the "bottom falling out" is comfortable and elusive. I claim I've worked for myself. This is another lie. I've rarely done anything for myself. It was always for others. Here I am lying again. Where do I gather the gall to even remotely assume everything I've done is for someone else? Although she was a burden to me, my daughter slowed me down. Even though I was a drunkard, I accomplished socially acceptable goals.

I've strayed again. The second shot ricocheted into

the next apartment. This apartment housed a young mother and three children under the age of four. The police were called. I was taken to jail. That was the most logical solution to the problem, for I was totally out of control. It is only through God's grace, that it was an overnight stay. My daughter was gone when I arrived home that morning. She'd called the aunts in Cleveland for help. My sister was also visiting family in Cleveland. She knew I drank too much. My aunts knew I drank too much and alcoholically. Apparently, they'd reassured my daughter of their continued support. She needed that. I was unreliable, just as my mother had been throughout my childhood and beyond. The truth hurts and heals simultaneously.

-It's Because of God's Grace That I live and Breathe Today-

Booze had turned me into an animal, or better still, I was already an animal, booze just brought the beast to the surface. I was a cruel, hardhearted beast. I secretly hated my daughter, because I felt incapable of love or being loved. I believed my daughter stood in the way of my progress. The reality of the situation was my alcoholism, turned everything good in my life into ugliness. My daughter stabilized me. She served as the thrust for all the goals I'd accomplished in my lonely life. She kept me out of the penitentiary. Why did I despise her so? She was my flesh and blood. I took such good care of her as a baby. My daughter never had a diaper rash, cold or ran a temperature. This is the honest truth. My drinking escalated, shortly after she turned three in 1977.

How have you abused your children?

_____

_____

_____

_____

_____
_____
_____
_____
_____
_____
_____
_____
_____
_____
_____
_____

JAMES
8/14/94

James (Puddin's father), was the perfect man to impregnate alcoholic me. Why did I choose him? I was afraid of men. The sexual abuse episodes in my life, left me scarred. James was puny, handsome and carried a badge. In the beginning, I thought he was wonderful. I remember so little- it was those alcoholic blackouts. We met at Kent State University, October 1971. Because of an alcohol related incident, he had been fired from Kent State, but that's his story. I was already a full blown drunk. It hadn't occurred to me to watch the signs. The blackouts, trouble, remorse, irresponsibility, lies, indiscriminate sex, pills and lascivious behavior were normal and unchecked.

So, I choose this married, smiling man to father my child. My emotional and old-fashioned thinking convinced me this was the way to keep a man. When we met, I was but a child, barely seventeen. What could be so far fetched? The next step was to drop out of school. James and I moved to a small apartment in Fairborn, Ohio. I, who was raised fatherless and literally motherless, will now tell you why I thought a helpless baby would solve my problems. My mother had three children by married men. I am the oldest. The only father figure I remember was the man who fathered my brother and sister. This man in his own perverted way loved my mother. He was with her as much as possible. They were two drunks who I believe really loved each other. My mother was very happy when she was in the company of my brother and sister's father. Booze kept them together and separated them. At times, he'd break into our shack, beat her, and demand instant sex. She always obliged. I recall fights, fucking and partying. I hated him. I don't understand this kind of love. However, instant sex, whether I liked it or knew about it, saved my life on many an occasion.

I assume my inability to trust was caused by betrayal in childhood. The loneliness of my childhood and despair of my drunkenness make it almost impossible to form a true partnership with another human being. Today I remind myself that I am worthy of love. They answers are within me, if I only look. Pull back the curtains of hate, anger and fear and look. There is beauty and peace behind them.

-At first I thought my inability to trust was caused by childhood betrayals.-

God please, please give me the strength and willingness to pull back the curtains. Please give me the courage to look. Living in the real world; the sober world is weird and wonderful. This world isn't skewed by alcohol. A world that is plain, bittersweet and visible. The world that wants fellatio just as men do. Today, I'll take life straight without any chaser. Life is caressing my clitoris and readying me to orgasm in its beautiful mouth. O O O O H!!! **Let the fun begin!**

Use various metaphors to describe "life"

RAMBLINGS
8/19/94

The apartment complex I lived in after the Parkside projects and before I brought this Yalecrest house, was managed by a slumlord. He collected rent and performed as few maintenance repairs as possible. The building was peopled by mostly drunks and junkies. I read somewhere that people take things which aren't protected. My childhood is proof of this. I had to protect my home. Why can't someone protect me? I'm always the strong one? I know I'll recover on a daily basis. I will recover from the fear of my breasts falling off. That's an interesting tale. It's odd how it came up. My femininity has always been at odds with my perceived self.

After Lamar, Andrew and others, I began to wish I were a "boy." As a young teenager, I ordered Charles Atlas books. I wanted to be as strong as a man. I didn't want men to hurt me anymore. With strength, I could pulverize and kill them. In my world, women were constantly mistreated. The woman I saw abused the most was my mama.

My mother was beautiful. Wilma was tall, slender and heavenly of face and figure. Her soul was tormented. Her release from self came by way of alcohol and sex. Gilmore was her man. His middle initial was "B." As far as I was concerned, it stood for "beast." He would beat her ass and afterwards they'd fuck.

-My mother was beautiful-

It made no difference if the children were present. I saw my mother fuck on many occasions when I was in Alabama.

Where's the nice man who'll keep me safe and out of harms reach? He was nowhere to be found. So Charles Atlas became my hero. The ripping, bulging muscles made him appear strong and able to kick ass. I was an avid comic book reader. His ads were in comic books. Shortly, after I turned twelve, I started my menstrual cycle.

The Charles Atlas ads seemed to leap from the page at me. Somehow, I saved my nickels and dimes and ordered his body building book. When the muscle book arrived, I was ready. Fresh into puberty, I was caught off guard. The book wasn't working, but my ovaries were. I was menstruating. I'd read about "it" in Cleveland's gigantic downtown library. This library was fabulous. Because of it, my menstrual period was not totally a surprise. I, however, was deeply offended because none of the females told me about "it." In my mind, madness and ignorance are symbiotic. They fed off of each other at the exclusion of sanity and reason.

My dumb ass mammy and her sisters thought they were doing me a favor by shielding me from the flower of womanhood. Instead, their silence drove my paranoia to levels previously unknown. All I ever wanted was to be loved, cared for and adored. How in the hell could a descendant of the worst slave state (Alabama) in the confederacy want love and caring? How could I even understand it? Had I again lost my mind? How could I forget that my family suffered from the cancer of slavery? It penetrated their very marrow. Why blame the females? My aunts weren't prepared for menstruation either. My grandmother beat their asses when they developed breasts. No wonder they were afraid of their bodies. They thought something was wrong with them for growing "tits" and bleeding on a monthly basis. There nothing wrong with being a woman. Pray to accept your womanhood.

Pray for forgiveness. Pray for the courage to change. Pray daily and often.

My support group is wonderful. Sometimes I'll make coffee. This means I arrive early, make coffee and leave late. The simple things in twelve step groups such as hugs, handshakes, making coffee and emptying ashtrays serve to redirect my focus. It gets me out of "me." For sobriety to work it has to be shared. Making coffee is one of several strategies which force me to interact with people.

-It gets me out of "me."-

Because I have a selfish, self-centered and egotistical mind, I want everything to revolve around me. If you're a genuine asshole and want to stay sober one day at a time, try helping someone without expectation of payment. Thank God for twelve step programs.

Whom did you help today? What did you do?

_____
_____
_____
_____
_____
_____
_____
_____
_____
_____
_____
_____
_____
_____

JAIL
8/20/94

My Higher Power is my greatest asset today. As I formulate my concept of this Power, I grow more confident everyday. I will have everything I want in American society. What's mathematics? How does my fear of mathematics encourage feelings of inferiority? Who taught me to believe math was hard. Math is not hard. Math is what I make of it. When one thinks about it, all things have a logical mathematical foundation. My breathing, my walk, my rhythm are all based upon mathematics. I am mathematical. Today, I'll focus my attention on a mathematically based agenda.

The psychologist, Maslow had the theory half correct. Human beings are self-actualized only when they approach daily living holistically. This approach isn't limited to just social abnormalities and acceptance by groups. This holistic hierarchy's base must be grounded in spirituality. In striving toward a level of interdependence, a Higher Power is mandatory.

I am going to ask my Higher Power for what I want. This feels odd because of my polluted version of Christianity. I believe far too many religious lies. This takes me right back to the seriousness of my emotional twists. Here denial has been a positive crutch. The insulation denial provides helps me function. If I were exposed to the tremendous amount of psychological damage inherent in racism, I'd crack up. Denial has helped me pretend it's not there. Denial preserves my sanity.

My twelve step program offers me sober support along with other amenities. I heard yesterday all support groups have their origin in African spirituality. The rugged competitive notion of individualism is discarded in such programs. They are termed "we" programs. Let it be known that infusing this new ideology into the psyche is a process, not an event. Let me tell you how fear locked me up again.

Living in my Parkside housing project, required three skills: an ability to fight, an ability to ignore the abject poverty that surrounds you and if you're a drunk, the ability to interact safely with criminals of all assortments. The last tool, if you will, calls for being placed in many life threatening situations.

-SOBRIETY IS A PROCESS NOT AN EVENT-

In my heart, I wanted people to respect and admire me. I longed for them to look up to me. I was a raging drunk-how could they? The fears I felt when sober, vanished into some unknown recess of my being during drunkenness. The false courage supplied by booze was incredible.

I was drunk that night. I was in an alcoholic blackout. I remember bits and pieces of that shadowy night. Earlier that day, I hooked up with Joetta and Joyce. Joetta drank more than me. I thought I was better that she. On the other hand, Joyce was more a dope fiend than alcoholic. Joyce liked women. She turned me on to crack that night. Joyce wanted my body. When I drank, I had multiple sex partners-men and women.

Sobriety checks all my bestial and irrational sexual perversions. I know where the perversions have their origin. I know why they grew in me. Mama, I always wanted the love of my mama. The three of us had been drinking and drugging for hours on end.

Because of my low self-esteem, I played Miss Bigtime and supplied dope and spirits. Why not, I was getting the attention and obeisance I longed for. Money buys false friends. It always has, it always will. If you're a fool, you're just that-a fool! These Judas' were sucking up my booze and dope. Music, laughter and nonsensical scavengers soon surrounded me. When all the dope was smoked and all the booze was drunk, when that was all gone- so was my "court."

I was a courtless queen sitting in a roach-infested project kitchen, angry and broke.

All of a sudden, evil welled up in me. I went berserk. My favorite night stick or "niggah stick" was used to bludgeon my kitchen furniture. I beat Joetta and Joyce with the stick. In my hot and frenzied mind, voices screamed "they're using you." I couldn't have that. Not after all the money I'd spent. I was out of my mind- insane! I don't recall when the police arrived. Neighbors told me, I attempted to attack one of the police officers. Somehow, I was subdued. It didn't take much to overpower me. Alcohol made me weak not strong. The police took me to jail. That's where I belonged -behind bars.

The following morning, the Iceman posted bail and picked me up. Without him, I was a full-time, round the clock drunken pauper. One the way home, everything looked bleak and dull. I felt drained and lifeless. Iceman and I made the short journey in complete silence. When we arrived at 1208 Lima Place, Parkside Homes, I climbed onto my small couch. In the cell, my bed was a brick slab. It was ice cold and blanketed with pungent reality. Thank God for my friend and lover, Iceman. He was a real disciple- a Moses of sorts. Although he was a heavy drinker, he was not alcoholic.

My mind and body had once more endured one of the worst drunks in months. Iceman left, I'd see him later in the evening. Alone on the couch, I hurt. It was a deep hurt. Tears never crossed my putrid mind.

-AN OUT OF CONTROL DRUNK MUST BE LOCKED UP-

Remorse was nowhere in my vocabulary. I hurt because booze was slowly cutting my esophagus and stomach to shreds. My stomach was leaking acid into places where it should not have leaked. I lay on the couch twelve or fourteen hours. This respite tempered my stomach fire. Once again, I'd spent another beautiful, sun kissed day sick, guilty and alone. A beautiful day in the crevice of my Parkside living room. A beautiful day without seeing my daughter's smile or feeling her warm caress. A beautiful day shot to hell. A beautiful day gone- gone to the dogs. Forever gone! Gone, because my alcoholic hell was more important than freedom, blood, sunshine, food, lover or anything else. Later that night, I was again ready for alcohol. Iceman arrived as agreed upon. Once again, I was off to the races. I speeded headlong into another homemade hell.

Use the lines below and describe how drinking has affected your physical health.

_____

_____

_____

_____

_____

_____

_____

_____

_____

_____

_____

_____

_____

_____

_____

THE ICEMAN
8/21/92

I learned to play golf because as an undergraduate, I majored in Health and Physical Education. Golf was one of several electives needed to complete my Bachelor's degree.

Alcoholism would bury my golf skills for over fifteen years.

A fair-weather girl-friend, Tonya and I were fucking the same man. This man enjoyed the game of golf. He was a married whore and thus unavailable for anything other than drinking and fucking. He drank alcoholically. He was what gals and guys call a "pretty niggah." The Iceman was the handsome man's uncle.

Everyday after playing eighteen holes, the golfers would drink in the parking lot of Madden Golf course in Dayton. Since she was familiar with the negro golf elite, I asked Tonya which golfer made the most money. The man who would later be known as the "Iceman" was introduced to me as Coleman Cummings. He was the "daddy" I always longed for.

The year was 1977. He was a General Motors executive. He was an above average golfer and thirty-two years my senior. Talking about Iceman is paradoxical. On the one hand he was my best friend, on the other- my greatest enabler. Today, I am grateful for both roles.

Iceman was raised by his grandparents. He was born in state of Kentucky, where Jim Crow and segregation were the norms. Iceman was raised to obey whites. His upbringing kept him alive. His grandparents knew he'd be lynched if he acted as though he was equal to whites. He lived to graduate from high school in the south. He first worked as a janitor with General Motors. There he took advantage of training and educational opportunities offered by GM. He completed both undergraduate and graduate school and was slowly promoted up the corporate ladder. I met him when he was but a few years from retirement. The Iceman was the king of heavy drinkers. He rarely staggered. His temperament remained constant. He was cool under pressure. He devoured a good time. I was already straddling the invisible line of alcoholism. There were days when I didn't remember anything. "Blackout City" should have been my name.

Iceman possessed the quiet confidence of one who is loved by God. He wasn't one to talk about religion. He literally lived the blessed life. It seemed to me all his prayers were answered. He was an old, powerful, empathetic and non-judgmental whore.

Although married, he'd lived with the "other woman" for over a decade. They had a son together. The mother of his bastard son found out about us. We were golfing in Florida. He was playing golf. I was making a complete fool of myself, drinking and such. While in Florida, the other "other" woman called. She told him he wasn't welcome in her home anymore. Who gives a fuck! Neither of us was wedded to him. Plus, he'd been juggling women for years.

It was only in the last years of his life, that I knew him to spend time with his "lawful" wife. What a woman the wife must be. Either giving him unconditional love or completely insulating herself from his wanderings. Whatever, I don't envy her position. I understand it not. It's a wonder that old fart lived through it all. That's another story altogether.

Before the Iceman, I rarely dressed like a fashion plate. The usual welfare attire was enough. Most of my clothes before Iceman were from thrift stores and or given to me. The old blouses, old skirts, cheap shoes and clean underwear were the usual trappings. With Iceman, I dressed! For years I was one of Dayton's welfare fashion plates. My figure is still fantastic. Tight dresses and high-heeled shoes were my weapons. Long, pretty wigs and plenty of make-up adorned my head and face. Beautiful coats and all sorts of "nigger" jewelry completed the look. "Nigger" jewelry is those earrings and bangles that are bigger than one's hand.

Although destructive, alcoholism served to insulate me from overt racism. It helped me pretend racism was non-existent. What a miserable joke I played on myself. Once again I felt God's grace. Grace was always a part of my essence, yet blinded by booze, dope and hate, I was unable to see it. I stayed drunk, drunk, drunk! Years came and went. I noticed few if any changes in my external or internal conditions. My daughter grew up in front of my eyes. I remember bits and pieces of our volatile, unloving relationship. My life revolved around playing big shot with an old man. It meant more to impress others than care for my own flesh and blood. With my self-esteem as high as a pregnant snake's belly, what else was I supposed to do?

It takes courage to look within. It takes willingness and the desire to confront the undisciplined self. This was what I blinded myself against. No way was I going to become introspective and challenge long accepted, outdated ways of thinking and living. I'd been ripe for alcoholism since childhood. There were so many horrifying issues I ran away from.

If alcoholism is to work, denial is a must. I must constantly deny the truth. So here's a beautiful lady with a pretty daughter on welfare in a housing project. I was as ripe as an egg halfway between menstrual cycles. All it took was the flash of dead presidents; along with a kind touch and I'd give birth to drunkenness. The Iceman had both. Since I was all but frigid, sex didn't mean much to me. Sex like so many other things, was a tool. I used it as needed. Because I believe I wasted many precious years I'd chide myself to no end. God help me. I will console myself by believing that today is the best day of my life. On a daily basis I am learning to rid myself of the forces of self-destruction which reside in me.

I'm confident enough today to pray for willingness and acceptance. It means looking within while reaching out. I'm still working on this date, August 21, 1992. The diaries I've maintained hold so much recovery minded truths. Keep the focus on Queen. Acceptance is the key to all my problems today. While checking my diary's pages, Barbara and Travis reared their ugly heads. I met Barbara D. and family my first few months in Parkside.

Describe instances when you used sex as a weapon or a tool which kept you safe among dangerous people or in dangerous places.

_____
_____
_____
_____
_____
_____
_____
_____
_____
_____
_____
_____

BARBARA
8/21/92

Barbara was one ugly, black, nappy haired, funny bodied bitch. She had reason to be jealous of me. Like my mother, Barbara had three children. My mother had children by two married men. Barbara had children by three unmarried men. This is another carryover from slavery-babies fathered by several men. Like me, Barbara was from Alabama. Her building was perpendicular to mine. Barbara's old man, Melvin, was an abuser. In many ways, their relationship mimicked my mother's. Ugh! Nasty! Could it be that was what drew us into a friendship? No, that's another lie. We were alcoholics. We drank together. We would drink in my apartment. Upon returning home, Melvin would beat her mercilessly. She'd remain with him.

Barbara had a son named Travis. As a child, he giggled whenever I was near him. He'd lived on welfare all of his childhood and most of his teenage years. Like many black males, the fast drug money reeled him in. The money represented freedom from want. It meant "power." Travis became a drug dealer. He was later shot and jailed.

When Travis, the man, first made a pass at me, I ignored him. I was afraid of his mother, Barbara. This drunk had gone to a twelve step group and gotten better. She sobered up. Her sobriety lasted several years. All of a sudden, she was drinking again. I had long since stopped associating with her. It wasn't long before Travis was paying me hundreds of dollars for sex and more. Neither he nor I cared that I was sixteen years his senior. Boy did we have fun!

Mama's niggah's name was Willie B. Gilmore. My mama wouldn't leave Gilmore until the state threatened to take us away. To escape that threat, we moved to Cleveland. Gilmore's name is synonymous with abusers. My mama was madly in love with him. To me, it seemed he was always lurking near by. My mama and Gilmore were two trifling fuck-ups. They were in love with each other. He was the only man I recalled my mother spending time with. Gilmore scared me so. He was mean to me. He caused ill feelings to grow between my brother, David and me.

When parents "favor" certain children, the other siblings always remember it. Gilmore would give David candy and instruct him to not share with me. David loved his "big" sister. He'd risk ass whippings from Gilmore to share with me. On the other hand, I rarely shared with him. I hated my brother because he was male. He would one day become a man. I saw men as abusers. They hurt women. They hurt my mama. They hurt me. In my world, women were victims.

At the age of nine, I sought to counter this treatment. I'd attack and beat my brother. My intent was to instill fear. If he feared me, he wouldn't hurt me when he became a man. I had no mercy or trust in men. This ideology persists unto this day.

Write your thoughts about what you've just read?

_____

_____

_____

_____

_____

_____

_____

_____

_____

_____

ACCEPTANCE
8/22/92

What's acceptance all about? It's simple to say. It's easy to do. The key to acceptance is to develop an open mind. An **open** mind is flexible. An open mind is trained to work in the best interests of its owner. Only then can I become willing. I can become willing to grow and become the best I can be.

My twelve step group uses a popular affirmative statement. Here it is: **"God grant me the serenity to accept the things I cannot change; courage to change the things I can; and the wisdom to know the difference."** Let's dissect these mighty words. Serenity means calmness and tranquility. Accept means to see, to receive favorably.

Courage is an attitude of dealing with difficult and dangerous things without running away. These "things" can be real or fancied. Wisdom is following a right and sound action plan.

I want to accept myself-the way I am now. I want to focus on self-understanding. This happens when I quit trying to fix everyone else. When I concentrate on Queen and her upkeep, there's no time for "fixing" anyone else. The job of introspection is huge.

Drunks and dope fiends are people users and excellent leeches. We live in a world of denial, anger, resentment and low self-esteem. We intentionally and confidently manipulate enablers who really love us. These enablers love us unconditionally. We repay them by roaring through their finances and lives without the slightest remorse.

In truth, our enablers hurt and pain only spurs drunks on. We treat them more merciless and with greater contempt. It's similar to the master-slave relationship; Black Americans are still struggling with today. No matter how the slave pleased the master, she was always despised. The same with enablers.

In recovery, impatience is a death knell. Like alcoholism, recovery must be merciless. It must track and strangle the disease of alcoholism just as a constrictor snake would its desired prey. Living sober is not a game. Wellness is not a quick fix. I had to realize others saw changes in me before I recognized them. Through unrelenting prayer, I slowly began to see changes. Other changes were imperceptible, but significant.

I'm glad I know how to read and write. Reading and writing has brought to light new and interesting worlds. I think about those marvelous ancestors who never touched a book. Those ancestors who were mutilated if caught touching books. I think of the illiterate, brainy and brave souls who taught themselves to read and write. I know not their names, but their blood runs through my veins. I think about how slothful so many black youth are today-they don't want to read and write. How sick!

Thank you Higher Power for sobriety today. Thank you, for this precious gift of life. Each day I am sober, I am paying a tribute to the slaves' courage and sacrifice. I will reach my goals via sobriety, one day at a time. I will not again kill myself today.

-Drunks and dope fiends are unsurpassed people users and master manipulators-

I will live today. I will help at least one soul today. By God's grace, I'll be the light at the end of my tunnel. Remember this Queen when you feel like its useless-God doesn't make junk. Because of sobriety, I can choose today. My sobriety frees my ass. Remember the old saying "free your mind and your ass will follow." Today I choose life.

This great country is still engaged in a pandemic alcohol and drug war. The effects and casualties of this war make all wars of the last 150 years seem like child's play. In conventional war death represents finality. The alcoholic war leaves the victim alive but lifeless. They are thinkless and thankless. This war rages within the sufferer. They become the walking dead. Like energy the God Force cannot be destroyed. Believe me; it's in all of us. It will never leave us. We must call upon this force on a daily basis. Continue to pray and you will find yourself instinctively seeking out positive connections which will guide you in self-discovery and recovery. As we learn to accept things as they are, we automatically reject bullshit.

We must ask the God of our understanding to forgive us for our lack of faith and impudence. Higher Power please protect me from cigarettes, drugs and booze today. Protect me from the self-destructive forces that jockey for first place in the recesses of my neurotic mind. Help me remember excuses are just reasons to pick-up. Alcoholism can be only be arrested there is no cure. The times I've been arrested were during intoxication. Other than that, the police don't bother me. When drunk, I subconsciously seek help through arrest. The arrest is a form of salvation. A violent, blackout drunk who doesn't get arrested usually wreaks serious havoc during a drunken episode.

Arrest isn't the answer, but once I singlemindedly turn myself into a raging animal- what's left besides jails, insanity and death. Treatment is effective when the debased drunk wants it to be effective. It works when you work it. Acceptance of the powerlessness and unmanageability of alcoholism is a must. One day at a time, I accept my alcoholism. One day at a time I'm free to live, grow and become a useful human being. Sobriety, one day at a time!

SISTER ANN
8/23/92

Cleaning my side of the street also meant expunging a misdemeanor criminal offense. Throughout this brief journey in sobriety, I've had the pleasure of making many acquaintances. I met Sister Ann while working towards my Master's degree. She was born in the former British colony of Uganda. She was the prototype of the British educated scholar. All "t's" crossed and "i's" dotted. She is one of the remarkable selfless members of the human race. Sister was angry and silent. Her writing and reports were sterile and lifeless. I on the other hand, wrote with vibrato. The professors knew my writing. My words pricked their consciousness and stimulated thought. Sister and I started meeting in the library. We helped each other. What a pair!

As a child she was reared as a stanch, strait-laced Catholic. The church agents and missionaries robbed

Uganda of its wealth with a Bible in one hand and gun in the other. Thus sister was confused. Like the American descendants of slaves, she lived a double life. She embraced the love of humankind, yet detested the rape of her beloved Uganda. Sister was frustrated because Catholicism was the bastard child of a religion which stressed a double standard.

Throughout graduate school I was angry and very vocal. I criticized the educational system because of its political undercurrents. I was frustrated because education wasn't working for a great many children, particularly those with slave ancestors. The public schools were crumbling from the inside out. I'd suffered under the hypnotic effect of public education. At that time, my thinking wreaked of a defeatist ideology. Realizing my thirst for knowledge wasn't slaked by universities, I gave up on education. Who needs education when a drink or drug is only a cough away? This attitude proved to be a "cop out." Since God loves me, I'm revamping this philosophy.

This selfishness, dishonesty, resentment and fear will be placed in their proper perspective. Socially I was a misfit. I hid behind drunkenness to avoid developing constructive relationships with people. I was only happy when I was in an alcohol induced blackout. Thus when I became involved in the community's infrastructure, I was overwhelmed to say the least.

Before God sobered me up, I'd been involved along the fringes of the community's skirt. I was scared to stand out and scared to stand up. Afterall, most people I associated with knew me to be a serious and unstable drunk. Alcoholic is a glitzy word. I was a drunk. I fucked up constantly. As a result, word got around that I was a pure, black asshole. Temperamental, clumsy, unreliable and untrustworthy-I was pathetic. Only by God's grace am I sharing with you today. Thanks God! Thanks Higher Power!

You see, without God's Grace, I'd still be a drunken slut. It is only because of my resurrection that I even considered attending graduate school. It is because of sobriety I earned my master's degree.

What goals have alcoholism kept you from reaching? Are you willing to persist until you get what you want?

_____

_____

_____

_____

_____

_____

THE SIXTH FLOOR
8/23/92

After fifteen plus years in Parkside, and before the house on 5103 Yalecrest Drive, I moved to Lantern Arms. It was a high-rise apartment building about a half-mile west of downtown Dayton. There's a park across the street and a scenic view of the Miami River less than a stone's throw away. My crib was easily accessible from interstate I-75. A gorgeous tree stood majestically outside my kitchen window.

The place used to be riddled with drunks, dope fiends (me included) drug dealers and crack-cocaine whores. The derelicts one comes to associate with the foul, filthy stench of alcoholism, addiction and abuse lived here. The manager was a drug dealer. Drugs deals and drunks were residing on each of the six floors. It was a vertical Parkside Homes. Lantern Arms had been raided several times. When the first bust went down, I was still using and drinking. It never even once crossed my mind that I was part of the problem in those apartments. By the time of the second bust, I was sober and clean.

I lived on the sixth floor. There were times when I

would get drunk and high in my neighbor's apartment. This malicious friend had two dogs and two cats. One dog was old as Methuselah. The other was Methuselah's twin. The cats were pissing and shitting all over the apartment. The dogs were allowed to defecate on the balcony. Of course this posed a health hazard, but I didn't care.

Methuselah was named "Chico." He smelled. Chico was rarely bathed. His owner would pile clothes in a corner near her clothes closet. There Chico would rest and piss. With so much drug traffic running in and out, I'd make myself comfortable in "Chico's" corner. From that filthy pile of dog clothes, piss, etc., I'd shell out 'C' note after 'C' note. Since I hadn't learned to buy dope, Chico's owner, Betty, would rip me off unmercifully. She'd return with less than my money's worth. I'd then proceed to give most of my dope away. I wanted them to like me. You see, drunks and dope fiends are very insecure. This insecurity stems from deep self-hatred, self-loathing and anger. *I was very insecure*.

My understanding of self at the time demanded I throw lavish drug and booze parties. Six and seven hundred dollars nightly on dope and booze adds up. This is what I did. Religiously, I'd lie, hustle, con and steal for booze and drug money. My low self-esteem was always active. I reasoned if I entertained these people, they'd like me. For some ludicrous reason, I desperately wanted everyone to like me.

There's that alcoholic grandiosity sneaking in again. My body and mind was one big painball. I hurt all over. Thus, when I sobered up, many drunks and druggies were still active in the apartment building. Doors and elevators were opening and closing throughout the night. Drunks and dope fiends prowl like wild carnivores. They thirst for the flesh and blood of those who will cater to their alcoholic and drug induced whims.

After sobering up, I soon tired of living like a fugitive in my own apartment. The cops had busted the building a few weeks earlier. Nonetheless, drug activity resumed with the strength of ammonia backing it. Drunks and crackheads loitered in the building's entrance, lobby, stairwells and hallways. I was tired of the shit. Therefore when my Higher Power dressed me in a protective suit of sober armor, it was time to go to work.

Fearless, reckless and without forethought, I contacted the owner and manager respectively. The owner of the building was a "pussy" and only interested in the rents being collected in a timely manner. That was until the city of Dayton threatened him with another drug bust. There was a new city ordinance, two busts in two years and you're out of business. The second bust would've shut down the property for two years. This new threat forced the owner to fire the drug pushing manager and evict troublemaking drunks and druggies.

Next, I sought help from the neighborhood priority board and neighborhood tenant association. The priority board representative attended our building's neighborhood meetings. The area neighborhood association began to meet in Lantern arms. The remaining tenants were pleased with the results and some became active in the tenant's association. Let it be known, none of the changes were smooth. At times, it was like running through cold molasses. There were rocky roads. Why shouldn't there be? What fun is there when everything is without effort and sweat? In short for over a year, the Lantern Arms Tenant Association was a strong presence in the building and surrounding area. Today, there isn't a manager on the premises. I'll move in a couple of months. I'm buying a house.

How did you help destroy your neighborhood?

_____

_____

_____

_____

_____

_____

_____

_____

_____

_____

_____

CONTEMPLATION
8/25/92

The revolution occurs in my mind. It involves all parts of it. It's a holistic approach, designed to help me find my God. This God of my understanding lives! Sobriety is effective when I examine the entire self- financial, intellectual, social, emotional, physical (including sexuality) and spiritual parts of my being. I like to look fabulous. Therefore, the physical is very important to me. Let me tell you about a fat liar. You see honey, denial is a sickness. Like alcoholism, it never sleeps, always patient-always waiting to strike.

One of the tenants in Lantern Arms claimed she'd had enough of drugs and alcohol. She looked like the Pillsbury doughgirl in blackface. Experience had taught me to proceed with caution with her kind. They are undisciplined people and deserve their misery.

Obesity like alcoholism requires effort, determination and denial. It too is caused by emotional disturbances. In fact, the same disturbances-fear, anger and low self-esteem which fuel drunks and dope fiends. Both are illnesses, both kill. Anyhow, "Fatty" chose to do it her way. She made excuses, ate like the pig she was and stopped exercising. These same excuses helped her gain an additional twenty pounds of lard. Last seen, she was watching T.V. and munching a bowl of party mix. Well, my Higher Power didn't give up on me. I'll continue to pray for her success.

Denial is a very intricate, but simple defense mechanism. It relies completely on its hosts desire to remain blind. For instance, everytime I'd get into trouble, I was intoxicated and drunk out of my mind. Thank you Higher Power. Although somewhat lacking in confidence, I'll continue to walk through the fear until I break free. So they say acceptance is the key to all my problems and concerns. I'll continue to pray for the bastards and me.

I must be free of tortuous jealousy, low self-esteem and fear. All are children of anger. Once again, it's important for me to attend the meetings. The meetings are seeped in holistic concepts which underscore African systems of spirituality. Why must I start to whine? Here goes! I always wanted to please my mama. I never knew my father. As a child, I never questioned her. It came to me during active alcoholism that she was a sick woman. My oppressive family and this sick culture eventually killed her. I am rising above mediocrity today. The ancestors are watching over me.

Mama told me I couldn't sing. My voice is a beautiful many stringed instrument. I can imitate the roar of a lion, buzz of a bee, song of a bird or the coo of a baby. The maddening thing about my mama is I believed everything she told me. Parents have so much power. Somewhere in my upbringing, I learned to respond after a single reproach from my mother. Therefore, I only needed to hear "you can't sing" just once. I believed her. This belief still persists to this day. However, I raise my voice anyway. I am going to break free. My voice is beautiful. I started weekly singing lessons in the fall. They were interesting and enjoyable. Country music was my preference. There are few black women in country music. There are a very few black males, Cleve Francis and Charlie Pride instantly come to mind. My plans call for revamping my goals and priorities. Although singing is low on the totem pole, I'm going to continue my lessons. I can sing. My voice is beautiful. My throat is clear. It seems all black folks know is how to be humble and cow tow, especially the older generations.

In August 1992, I was ten months sober. I felt excellence could be achieved by staying sober one day at a time. I was giving teaching second thoughts. I felt consulting was more profitable and would utilize my time more effectively. Now I realize I'm destined to become a competent and highly compensated public speaker.

Self honesty and acceptance of unmanageability are vital and necessary for growth. I am growing up. It's about fuckin' time. The men I have a preference for in sobriety tend to have these characteristics. They are submissive, of average intellect and income. Most are and shorter that me and have poor listening skills. The above was what I looked for after ten months sober. My cleansing process was slow- just my speed at the time. Here's my current description of my dream man.

He's black, broad shouldered, six feet plus, smart and his pockets are lined with money. My man is booze and drug free and has a concept of God. My man is protective and fearless. He uses all of his intellect and power for teaching and self-affirmation. My man-friend appreciates the gift of life and guards it fiercely. He's a splendid sex partner and in excellent health. I'm always satisfied. If the above is immature, then so be it.

Higher Power help me today. Help me walk through my fear, anger and low self-esteem. I believe you've always been with me. Through thick and thin, we've always been together. I'm still on the subject of men. For years, I catered to shiftless, lazy men. I wrongly thought I could save them. Yuck-perish the thought.

Describe your dream man as of this moment.

_____

_____

_____

_____

_____

WORLD IN PALMS
8/27/92

Mahalia Jackson is singing. I'm writing. I love gospel music. It's deep and soul encompassing. Attending the library is also a way of life for me. The library is my ticket to the world's knowledge. Following convocation, the former president of Central State University, Arthur E. Thomas, would say - "go the library." During my tenure, he was Central State University's vice-president. Dr. Thomas never missed an opportunity to tell students about the treasures just waiting to be unearthed in the library. Although criticized for his dogmatic beliefs, he was kind to me. I saw him as a clear thinker and captivating leader. That simple directive still rings in my ears.

He introduced the speakers and closed the convocations. These convocations would motivate me. The words trickled from the lips of the world's greatest minds. Every now and then, an entertainer would sneak in and upset the momentum, but on the whole, great thinkers were heard. I was drinking heavily, so I attended convocations on an irregular basis. I missed many a grand convocation speaker because of drunkenness.

Alcoholism is such a pitiless thief. It ravages and destroys everything good and meaningful. Mama migrated north in late spring of 1966. I remember the time vividly because I missed the Maypole festival. This was the high point of the school year. It was a day of fun, food, festivities and ultimately goodbyes for sixth graders. In northern schools, I've seen nothing to rival Tuskegee's Maypole celebrations. The entire school looked forward to and participated in the Maypole revelry. This was an end of the school year celebration borrowed from our Irish slavemasters. During it, well-scrubbed, black children sang, danced and wrapped colorful ribbons around a long pole. The Maypole dance was performed by graduating sixth graders.

My initial exposure to libraries began in Cleveland, Ohio. The library held the keys to unlocking the mind. I believe in libraries. To this day, I visit the library at least twice weekly. When I'm working on a particular research project, I may visit three or more times in a seven day cycle. Dr. Thomas knew the importance of attending the library. He literally pleaded with students to visit the library. Although a drunk, who's now sober, I heeded his admonitions. The library is my friend, lover and companion. Within its doors I find answers to limitless questions. It was in the library where I tried to run away from booze and dope. I went there to find materials which would help me cope with subconscious denial. As far as denial goes, a drunk can use anything or anyone as an enabling tool. Yes dear reader, I will reiterate alcoholism and addiction are soul sicknesses. Denial is as necessary to addiction as breath is to life.

I stumbled across material by a doctor named Ari Kiev in the library. I hope you'll investigate his psychological theories. They are simple, yet thought provoking. I was a woman who'd been neglected by her mama. I'd given birth to a beautiful baby. I was an unfit mother. I felt failure caressing me. The one who was supposed to love me didn't. Thus, after reading Dr. Kiev, I still drank. Not only that but I was drunk and seriously believed I'd found a new way to drink without its sidekicks- trouble and pain. A perfect example of denial is knowing there's a problem, yet consciously ignoring the solution. The solution is to **stop** drinking. I wasn't listening to anyone who said "stop."

FOOT SOLDIERS
8/28/92

I never knew a daddy, or true love for a man. My half-ass mama overdosed. Family life was bleak to say the least. Why stop? I was a perfect candidate for addiction. It's a fact; the majority of people who have drinking problems are those with low self-esteem. I am going to pause here and thank my Higher Power. Without the gift of sobriety, I'd be unable to pen these thoughts and ideas. I'd be unable to assassinate the demons within today. Sobriety is a blessing. With it, I'll continue to accomplish great things. The world will know my name, Teresa Queen Johnson. The world will know of my adventures in the inferno of addiction. Talk about grandiosity!

Drunks will be helped by these writings. These new foot soldiers will take up spiritual arms and battle the foes within. The foes which compel us to destroy the self, reside within the self. The soul however can never be destroyed. Higher Power please take care of me. Protect me. Teach me self love. Thank you.

Describe how you will trust God today?

_____
_____
_____
_____
_____
_____
_____

_____

_____

_____

_____

SUPERFICIAL FAKES
8/29/92

Learning to listen requires commitment. It takes internal and external laser sharp focus and accuracy. Hearing and listening are miles apart. Here's the difference. When I hear, I remain the same. When I listen, I think. It's important I attend speaker type meetings in my twelve step group. When I attend these meetings, I do one of two things.

1. I do nothing and forget why I attended in the first place.
2. I listen and internalize precious tidbits that will accelerate the healing of my soul.

When I listen, it's critical that I sift through the debri. Debri are simple things which detract from my focus. Examples of debri are: exterior appearance, job status, social standing and income. Whatever superficial excuse I'm using to avoid looking into my soul is debri. It is soiled, unnecessary and must be discarded. Now I may be incapable of disposing of it immediately, but with acceptance of whom and what I am, I'll eventually rid myself of the damning burden.

Living and believing in a Power greater than Queen ought to be second nature. In reality, I've always had powers greater than myself. Let's look at several of those powers. I tend to be a clothes horse. When I dress, it's essential I turn heads and cause car accidents. I like to be razor sharp when I'm done dressing. I must be careful, for clothes too can become another of my gods.

The same goes for cars, fancy hotels and men. When I experimented with booze and dope, I had plenty of powers greater than me at my disposal. I was quick to run to another drunk or dope fiend and have them concoct a potion for me to ingest, smoke and or inhale. My dope and drink concoctions would get me high as I wanted to be. However, being a true drunk and fiend, I didn't know how drunk or high I wanted to get. I never got enough!!! The power I willingly assigned to booze and dope, was greater than I was. So why is it seemingly impossible to believe in a Power greater than myself today? It isn't.

I am immature emotionally, spiritually and socially. This immaturity causes me to act in childish and selfish ways. I excuse this malady in the personality by pretending it isn't there. This obstinate denial only serves to perpetuate the problem. What's the problem? When I drink, I get drunk. When I get drunk, I get in trouble.

My twelve step program, with its foundation in acceptance of a Power greater than me, helps me live sober on a daily basis. So can you. The loneliness of alcoholism can be handled in a constructive, rather than destructive manner. I am living proof, my Higher Power works in my life. I'm striving to become "honest," open-minded and willing.

Honesty is acceptance of my problem. Some call alcoholism a disease. It is a spiritual disease. It ravages the soul at the expense of the body. Now, I've already told you, the soul doesn't die. This is why tremendous guilt always followed my booze debacles. Guilt is the soul's way of getting attention. Without this form of consciousness, healing won't take place. For drunks and dope fiends, guilt demands recovery or death. It is always cut and dry.

Honesty even in its most primal form leads to open-mindedness. Learning to listen is a form of open-mindedness. Drunks and dope fiends tend to be close-minded. This close-mindedness is a form of denial. Its objective is to protect alcohol. Alcohol is the drunk's higher power. Honesty is the Siamese twin of acceptance. Open-mindedness is one's ability to listen. In time, willingness becomes automatic.

Through my twelve step program and acceptance of a Power greater than me, I live sober on a daily basis. So can you. **Honesty, Openminded** and **Willingness** are three important life changing words. It doesn't matter how the **HOW** is arranged. The words mean pretty much the same thing. Looking at my life and objectively questioning how drunkenness affected me in all areas is a necessity. The people I wanted to love, such as my family and daughter were affected. My income was affected. My emotions were dancing around like jumping beans. My physical and sexual lives were crumbling before my eyes. My attempts at living a "normal" life were impossible. Where was God?

Yes, my mama left the south permanently for Cleveland in 1966. Looking back on the trauma I was going through, it was a good decision. The cousins, trusted family males and other grown men were molesting me. I would've been pregnant shortly after beginning menstruation. Today I know my Higher Power intervened. I will be happy, joyous and free. I will keep coming back. I will trust the process. I will learn to live one day at a time.

List ten to twelve things, people and / or places you are grateful for?

_____

_____

_____

_____

_____

_____

_____

_____

_____

CINDERELLA, RELLACINDER
9/1/92

A Cinderella belief, such as I'll be able to drink like regular folks, is a myth. There are times when I like to relax with a book of fairy tales. I enjoy reading and letting my imagination soar. I even pretend I'm one of the characters.

Cinderella was majestic at the ball. Glass slippers, beautiful gown, sparkling jewels all adorned a svelte body. What a fairy tale! Cinderella never got drunk. Booze was never hinted at during the ball. So in my imagination this is what happened to Cinderella. First her fairy godmother was really a "fairy." Second the pumpkin carriage was a pimp mobile, a Cadillac, with lots of chrome. The sisters treated her cruelly because she tanned and they burned. The ball was really a showcase for whores who were eventually sold into slavery. I could go on and on. It doesn't take much to get off track.

The Cinderella story is a bizarre escape into the world of fairy tales and fiction. I believed in such tales most of my life. I actually believed I'd be rescued from all this chaos by a dashing prince on a white steed. It didn't matter that I was living a real Cinderella drama. So many things were occurring at the time. The poverty, abuse and neglect were a few of the conscious incidents.

During "drunks" and periods of prolonged intoxication, I'd pretend I was Cinderella. With my sugardaddy's help, I got all dressed up and pretty. To my way of thinking it never dawned on me that I was attracting sick, sick people. These people were trying to live out their own versions of the Cinderella story.

Ladies, gentlemen and friends of depressed drunks

everywhere, it gets better. If the desire is real, the desire to stop drinking is immediately followed by insight. At first, insight feels uncomfortable. It compelled me to seek out the people and tools which would strengthen my understanding of the Power. That Power which is greater than Queen resides in me. The feelings of uselessness and self-pity disappear because of this Power. The little, frightened girl in me needs to learn to love herself again. I am worthy. I deserve love. Self-acceptance and being true to my self are the keys. That's what Polonius said in Hamlet- "above all, to thine own self be true."

I'm also a Shakespeare buff. Lear, Macbeth and Hamlet are my favorite tragedies. In my opinion, they ended on a happy note. In King Lear, the seeds of jealousy destroyed Goneril, Regan and the envious brother. Pride killed Lear; ambition Macbeth and indecision Hamlet. All of the characteristics- jealousy, pride, and indecision can be traced to fear.

Good in each tragedy ultimately triumphed. Before the triumph of good however, chaos was prevalent and rampant. I wonder whether my twenty years plus of alcoholic chaos was the prelude to happiness and the triumph of "good." My troubles were basically created by my own hand. It's true; a life run on self-will can hardly be a success. There has to be a belief in a Power greater than myself. In short, this "power" automatically leads to a life which is logical, natural and harmonious. So why wonder? My Higher Power helps me understand negative ideologies, which have distorted my thinking. These warped ideas are present and inculcated in the ideologies of western culture.

As I was flipping through my notes, I happened upon a spicy tidbit of sorts. Throughout my mangled sort of thinking, I've wondered what to pray for. Some people caution against asking the Higher Power for anything except willingness to stay sober. Others say ask for what you want. Well, I'm definitely not at a loss for words here. In recovery, good things happen to me. The acceptance of alcoholism as something I'm absolutely powerless over prepares me for serenity throughout daily living. What after all is the Higher Power? The Higher Power is all that represents peace within the human soul. It is infinite. Every human being, I believe, is born with the Power. It cannot be measured or comprehended. Man in his finite understanding was given only an inkling of the Higher Power. Man's power to choose, is the closest comparison we have to the Power. The power to choose is a gift. Well, after subjecting me to such revolting experiences, you'd think I would have lost my mind by now, wouldn't you? No way!

What's your understanding of a Higher Power?

_____

_____

_____

_____

_____

_____

_____

_____

_____

_____

_____

_____

_____

_____

_____

_____

_____

ALLEY B.
10/5/92

I am free today. My Higher Power is based upon faith. Religion and faith are not Siamese twins. They aren't even on the same continuum. Great numbers of people are religious, yet have no faith whatsoever. They have no idea what faith means. Oh God, it's time to tell the tale of Alley B. On the last leg of my active addiction, I became involved with a "popper." That's what I call intravenous dope fiends. They're the ones who "shoot up." By the way, the last leg of my drunkenness spanned a period of five years.

Alley was in my life during the first two of those five years. To be more specific, he was "around" from 1986-1988. Alley was also a "gashman." He was a "cumfreak." That's a man who's a sex addict. He was concerned with his orgasms, never mine. As a matter of fact, he was upfront about it. He told me he was a "gashman." I thought I could make him love me. Here I was, totally incapable of loving myself and actually believing I could make a "junkies junkie" love me.

A "junkie's junkie" is the type of dope fiend; other dope fiends want to imitate. They do sick shit like steal meat from supermarkets and sell it for dope. Afterward, they go home, kiss their mama and when she turns her back, this vermin steals her bill money.

Alley asked me for a ride to a bootleg joint. I wanted his love and waited outside the joint for hours. While I waited, I was approached by unbeknownst to me, his partner. The comrade was also a junkie. He and Alley conned me. The comrade lied about a car part. If I give him money, it will be used for drugs. I gave the friend money for an alleged car part. He left. I waited and waited. Neither of the junkies returned.

The con works best when the relationship is fresh, within the first few weeks. Usually after sex has occurred. It's a test phase. The "j" junkie has to be sure she "qualifies." If she falls for the "car part" scam without leaving her car- she qualifies. This is a signal to the "j" junkie to continue the elaborate fabrications because she will comply with his twisted machinations.

A con only works if the mark is willing. I was willing. I was lonely and wanted to be liked and accepted by anyone. That's partially what happened with Alley and me. The crucial difference was he loved alcohol and drugs more than my delicious black cunt. On the other hand, booze and drugs were also my master.

Real drunks and dope fiends know how to make money. Regrettably it doesn't last very long. Alley had skills. He was a carpenter and brick mason. His masonry skills saw few rivals in Dayton, Ohio. His father was a contractor. His mother was a hard working insurance agent. He was reared in a beautiful two parent home. Yet, the things which went on in his home didn't leave me envious of Alley. Money covered up the debauchery that went on in that house. Mama and papa were constantly at odds. Alley wanted to shine in his father's eyes, yet he always fell short. No matter what he did, he just couldn't measure up in his father's eyes. It was rumored Alley was bisexual. The signs were there, I chose to ignore them.

I tried to imagine it wasn't so. Just as I ignored the warnings signs of my alcoholism; I also ignored Alley's homosexuality. He seemed to derive a pleasure from the company of men which wasn't apparent when we were together. The rumors persisted. Reality has a way of making the blind "see." Thus was the case with me. Alley went to shooting galleries and sissies followed him there. The galleries are dives where junkies shot dope into their veins.

Since Alley was a "junkies junkie," he had so called friends who'd let him use their "posh" apartments for his needs. By "posh," I mean there was electricity, running water and heat. He'd even dare to shoot up in his mama's house, on her bed and while watching her TV. She was working for money she knew he'd steal if given the chance.

Ms. Ora, his mother, was a great enabler. She denied anything was wrong with her son. Although the truth glared at her, she couldn't acknowledge he was ill. She too was sick. Believing she'd failed as a mother and wife, she showered her "fragile" son with material possessions. Like me, he sold everything valuable for booze and drugs. All drunks and junkies are thieves. We steal from low-risk weak people who love us. High risk people are those who'll kill us if we steal from them. Paradoxically, many high-risk people are those who abstain, yet supply the products. Because they understand the mindset of the drunk and junkie, they punish them severely when thefts are discovered.

Only the strong survive in the street. The people hanging out on street corners, doing personal favors, abusing children and themselves are losers. No matter what they say or how good the lie sounds, they are still losers. I lived the life of a loser for twenty plus years. I was blinded by denial, anger and low self-esteem. I chose men like Alley, James (daughter's father), Grego, etc. because I was living out a loser's life script.

You needn't live this way any longer. Help and hope is found within these pages. This book can help you come to believe in yourself. It's written to teach truth-very simple truths. The Power you so randomly seek is within you. It has been within you all along. Your destructive habits and manner of thinking were of your own making.

REBUILDING
10/5/92

The experiences of our childhood are vital and important. They subconsciously shape and mold our future. Adults who "cop out" remind me of myself during active alcoholism. They blame everyone and everything for their failures and apparent inadequacies. The last thing they want to do is look within for peace and serenity. So after years of hand picked hells, they find themselves backed into a corner. They either change or die.

Death masquerades in the form of denial, jails, institutions and death. Do you really want to die without having actually lived? Today, I've decided I'm going to use the necessary tools. These tools are freely given. Their function is to help me come to believe in a Power greater than Queen on a daily basis. After decades of alcohol and drugs being my Higher Power, I've accepted help. I am learning to look within for the answers. Go to the source of all power. That's you! Look within and begin using these simple tools. Humble yourself and pray without ceasing.

There are millions of drunks who've walked in your shoes and traveled the same road you find so crooked and rocky today. They're drunks and dope fiends who live without booze and dope. Just like we persisted in destroying our lives, we also persist in building new lives and attitudes one day at a time. Old things are passed away. Behold all things are become new. This is called a "psychic change." The change can't be bought, lent or hoarded. The change comes when we are of service to other sufferers. The question now becomes. "Am I willing to do what it takes to be free?" "Are my energies invested in staying sober today?"

Why am I all of a sudden thinking of slavery? I remember the childhood beatings with plaited switches, ironing cords, shoes and leather straps. I remember dangerous objects thrown at me. I remember the head to toe welts which resulted from the savage beatings mama gave me. These terrible beatings had been subconsciously passed from generation to generation. The intent was to make me "good." If I can be so bold as to assume in both the south and north being "good" meant obedience to white folks. If so, was I to become "good" from ill treatment? I live with many slave induced contradictions.

HOMECOMING
10/5/92

In September 1992, I was approaching my first year of sobriety. It was Central State University's annual homecoming. A dance was held in Dayton's swankiest hotel-Stouffers. I decided to attend this function solo. I experienced my first sober homecoming dance. I felt lost and out of place. This was one of many neurotic tricks I played on myself. Seeing through clear eyes is a blessing. It's different. I thought something was wrong with me. This, in truth, was just a trick. It was a trick played on me by my diseased mind. As long as I am without booze and dope, I feel awkward. The insanity of alcoholic thinking will always lurk within the wrinkled recesses of my being.

MORE JAMES
10/12/92

Let me share the ideology I used in choosing a father for my child. Most male figures in my life were cruel, mean and abused women physically and emotionally. I met a man. I only knew him briefly. I felt safe in his company. He treated me to McDonald's. We got drunk together. He was married with four children. I gave birth to our baby, another slave. Being a slave myself, it was easier to "do" than "think." However, there were times when my daughter's father was kind. He was a little thin man, but he'd stand up to the giants. The old fella had a lot of "heart." That's more than I can say for many a physically larger man. I don't know if it was the McDonald's burgers or the way he caressed my hands. It must have been the McDonald's because he was a lousy "fuck." We tolerated each other in a warped sort of way.

Why do I take more precious time thinking about my mama's ill treatment? Why think about post traumatic depression resulting from such treatment? Why think about the way she died-a prisoner of her mind. Why think about Brooklyn and the sexual molestations which took place at 288 Lafayette Avenue? Why think about my seven year old body being ravaged by grown men? Why think about the hunger and deprivation? Why think about the "aloneness" it all represented? Why think about the beatings and name calling? Why think at all? Get drunk, run away, but never, never think. Thinking is too hard.

I feel that even during the process of writing this book, I'm only scratching the surface of any real feelings. My feelings have been beaten so far into my subconscious, that when they emerge, they are always tainted with the poison of fear, anger and hate. Just for today, whatever it takes, I am going to stay sober, one day at a time. When I gave alcohol power over me, I made it my God. For years booze was more important than my own beautiful beloved daughter, health, safety, you or anything else.

I'm guilty and trying to make up for what I considered wasted time. It is time to be bold, bloody and resolute. When words of that complexion spill from the mouths of former drunken ex-slaves, others become frightened. Then again, with slavery still intact and stronger than ever, they may just laugh themselves silly. Afterall, I was a rather comic drunk, a regular stumbling, sad and pissy buffoon. America's population some sources say is ten to fifteen percent alcoholic. To this we add the three to four million crack and heroin addicts and you've got a mess. This "mess" is costing this country billions of dollars. It's regrettable that labor and manufacturing feel the brunt of this malady in lost wages and defective products.

The primary purpose of this book is to let you know there is a solution to your problem. What do I know? I am alcoholic. I will remain alcoholic until the day I die. My mind is constantly trying to trick me into believing I can safely drink. This is a bold-faced lie. For me, a real alcoholic, to drink is to sign my death warrant. I am a pseudo-slave. Yes, the physical shackles and chains are removed, but my mind is polluted with myths, lies and ghost goblin stories about the true meaning of God, happiness, sacrifice and salvation. Living sober on a daily basis is the first step in my physical and emotional catharsis.

1ST OMVI
10/12/92

In spring 1984, I was busted driving drunk. It was the best thing that ever happened to me. My daughter was nine years old and still sucking her finger. For me, my booze bottle sucking, like her finger sucking, represented my warped security blanket. My attorney asked the judge to send me to weekend intervention at Wright State University. In the intervention program, along with extracting hundreds of dollars for less than a forty-eight hour stay, they try to scare you sober. They showed gory films of traffic accidents where it seemed everyone in a one mile vicinity was killed. Diseased livers, hearts, brains, stomachs and other organs from alcoholic and junkie cadavers were readied for our hands on inspection. Everybody was sweating bullets. Big fucking deal, I reasoned, "I'm fine."

We all wanted to get drunk. We wanted to leave. This

wasn't possible. Technically we were under arrest until the program ended on Sunday afternoon. During weekend intervention, I admitted my powerlessness over alcohol. Yet the only God I had was that of my mother. This punishing, vengeful God wasn't working for me. When Sunday evening arrived, I was set "free." I sat in my car and cried like a baby. The seed had been planted.

Today in my twelve step groups, we believe the solution lies in the problem. So my ideology on the subject of God needed a complete overhaul. Off I went to the library. I searched rare and hard to find books. I traveled to storefront book stores. I traveled to different cities and states searching for answers. I interviewed men and women over seventy years of age. I theorized the elderly had a monopoly on God. I prayed for guidance. Soon the problem began to reveal the solution.

I was born with the spirit of God in me. In childhood, it is the parents' responsibility to nourish the good-force within the child. If children are abused, the God- force begins a period of hibernation. In this state, we travel in many pathways as we seek this Force which was always present in us. Because drunks and dope fiends are too busy foraging for things which keep them inebriated, they generally don't nourish themselves well. Most alcoholics are malnourished and dehydrated. I ate and drank well during that weekend intervention. Where did that come from?

FIRE HELL AND STONEBRIM
10/21/92

The travels of the drunk and dope fiend are synonymous with death. Acceptance and belief in the Power once more represents resurrection. Drunks and dope fiends who get and remain sober are resurrected from hell on a daily basis. The question now becomes "what is hell?" Hell is the attempted and willful destruction of the mind. Hell is an excuse. Hell is a cop-out. Through acceptance and sobriety there is no reason for any drunk or addict to live any longer in hell. Do you understand what I'm implying here? It's this, like sobriety hell is also based upon choice.

Today, I'm using my freedom of choice to liberate me from the mental shackles of alcoholic slavery. This is a process not an event. It takes patience and courage. Thus another objective in the sobriety curriculum is to develop patience and tolerance throughout the healing process.

It took years to become deathly sick. It will take years to recover. The years are the sums of days. I'm learning to live in the here and now one day at a time. Alcoholics must learn to come to grips with the full range of human emotion. Dr. Naim Akbar underscores the importance of learning history, painful or otherwise, and appreciating the strength and courage of the ancestors. In short, all Black folk have is emotion. Everything we do is emotionally laden. Dr. Akbar reasons blacks ought to place more stock and trade on solving problems using a scientific approach. I agree with this proposition.

Destructive behavior can be changed with this taxonomy. Let's take a look at the scientific method. What is the problem? I drink, take drugs and get into trouble. What have I done to get better? I've made thousands of excuses for my destructive choices. I haven't stopped making excuses. So I've really done nothing. Some say it's five, but for alcoholics there are only two steps. We learn more after acceptance of these two steps.

    1. Accept or reject being alcoholic
    2. Formulate conclusions and evaluate them.
Breakdown of Scientific Method
    A. What is the perceived concern?
    1. I drink too much!!!

B. Identify the real concern?
1. I might be alcoholic and therefore am unable to drink sociably, and without trouble, guilt or remorse.
   C. Assembling and classifying data and formulating hypothesis/theory (experiment)
1. Mixing together different solutions and concoctions designed to decrease or increase assimilation of booze and dope into the bloodstream, without the resultant trouble which by and large accompanies my drinking
   D. Nothing works
1. End up drunk
2. Drunk and in trouble
   E. Conclusions or end results of alcoholic drinking
1. Jails
2. Institutions
3. Death
4. Stop and permit your Higher Power to work in your life

In our nonstop search for discovery, let's pretend we're children more often. This is easy since a good number of drunks and dope fiends are infantile as it is. Children derive meaning from the world by exploiting all of their senses. Discover the joy of sobriety in a comparable way. Touch your children and other loved ones in ways which are tender and nonviolent. Introduce your nose to a mixture of smells both sweet fragrances and stinking ones with foul stenches. Taste a variety of bitter, sweet, sour and salty food. Visit different places and see things you've always dreamt of. Expose the skin to temperatures and textures that stimulate and refresh. Listen to sounds from the rush of running waters to the melodic reverberations of your sonata. If you aren't sure where to turn, make a beeline to your public library. It's the world at your fingertips.

I fear this question. What would you do with only six

months to live? How would you treat yourself? What would your obituary read? Sit down sometime within the next forty-eight hours and write your obituary. Be honest- do you want the words drunk, dope fiend, lush, dysfunctional parent, loathsome provider included in your writings?

Remember, denial is an emotion that's designed to shield our alcoholic and feeble egos. It is just as dishonest as alcoholic drinking. Denial chokes us and defends our living in our irrational booze and dope contaminated worlds.

Obituary

_____

_____

_____

_____

_____

_____

DEBACLE
10/13/91

My last debacle was abysmal. For sometime I knew I'd stop drinking or die. I just didn't know which would happen first- death or abstinence. In early October 1991, I'd been on several drunks, each leaving me sick and in a pained condition for days. The insidious insanity returned after the pain and sickness faded. I continued to drink as though impervious to all alcoholic dangers. My sugardaddy had left me. My daughter's father with the assistance of children's services had taken custody of her. My relatives wanted nothing to do with me. My so-called friends were in worse shape than I. I was in essence a scavenger- an eater of death.

I engaged in activities which used to repulse me. On that October morning, I'd pawned my pistol for several hundred dollars. I paid no bills. The thought never crossed my mind to pay bills with the gun money. I was going to get drunk and high.

As I turned the steering wheel of my Cadillac Deville, I thought of nothing but booze and drugs. My first stop was the "shooting gallery." This was the place where the most despicable souls carried out their inhuman existence with precise execution. They shot up and nodded from the heroin coursing through their bloodstreams. Their parasitic existence was balanced by thieves who waited for opportunities to steal not only money and drugs, but if need be - life itself.

I was compelled to play big time. My diseased mind craved subjects. I had a need to be looked upon. I had a need to be worshipped. It was not to be. First, I was already too drunk. Second, I wasn't familiar with this particular dive. I'd often passed the street on my way to my favorite watering hole, the Swat's club. I never stopped on this street. Today was different. This would be the day I said "good-bye," a day at a time, to a way of life which had become too painful and savage. In my soul, I knew it had to stop. I'd lost everything: daughter, jobs, significant others, money and most important, my self-respect. I pulled behind a beat up relic of a car which had several occupants in it.

Onlookers were standing around smoking, drinking and loud talking to each other. I stepped out of my caddy, trying desperately not to stagger. They looked. I liked that. Some of the "fiends" knew me from drunken exploits at bootleg joints. Some knew me from Parkside Homes. There were others who knew I was on my last leg in this drunken manner of existence. These were the ones I feared most. For these animals would buy anything I wanted. They'd help me drink and smoke it. Afterwards they'd crack my skull and leave me in a dark alley raped and or mortally wounded.

Subconsciously, I was suicidal and careless. Death

seemed inviting. If I were dead, I could not help others. If I were dead, I would have fulfilled a ghastly, self-fulfilling prophecy-you're just like your mother. I intended to kill myself. Thanks to my wonderful and merciful Higher Power, death would have to wait. I ventured into homes, cars and forbidden streets that last night in hell. I bartered away beautiful fourteen carat gold rings for a 'bump'. That's a teeny, tiny, itsy, bitsy small piece of crack cocaine. I then stood in an open alley, near a lighted street and engaged in fellatio for more crack. I was drunk, high and selling my precious soul for garbage. After the alley incident, I knew it had to stop or I'd die drunk. *At last, I had accepted that I was utterly alone. I had hit my bottom. I was ready for help.*

Somewhere, I don't know from whence it came, a voice said "go home." It was three or four in the morning. My car was nowhere to be found. I'd parked it somewhere and forgotten where it was. All the false friends were gone. The money was gone. I was alone again. This time, the "aloneness" was different. I felt odd and in a funny sort of way-relieved. It was as though something evil and wicked had been forced out of me.

Help appeared in the form of a benevolent man. His name was Herbie H., Out of the blue; I remembered where I'd left the Cadillac. He drove me to it. I thanked him and sped away. That evening I went and asked other sober drunks and dope fiends for help. AA men mostly were happy and thrilled I'd come back. The men were far kinder than the women. However, because of the Grace of a power greater than myself, I remain sober today.

Use the lines below and thank that "special friend." Believe it or not that person was sent by a kind and loving God.

_____

_____

_____

_____

_____

_____

_____

_____

_____

_____

_____

_____

_____

_____

_____

PARKSIDE NEIGHBORS
12/6/92

The retelling of my adventures and other tidbits is to help you craft and personalize your journey back to the realm of the living. In early December, 1975, I moved into Parkside Homes. My belongings consisted of two paper bags, my beautiful daughter and a lot of heart. I needed and took full advantage of welfare and its sparse offerings. If a single mother is smart and frugal, welfare can be a stepping stone to a better life. However, because of my addiction I was to reside in Parkside for over fifteen years.

I resided at 1208 Lima Place. Ruby Red was my next door neighbor in Parkside Homes. She lived at 1206 Lima Place. The slings and arrows of life in poverty left Ruby bitter and callous. She had two toddlers and was pregnant with her third child. She would eventually give birth to five children.

Ruby safeguarded herself from further hurt and psychosis with the poor woman's brand of defense. She cursed from morning to night.

In the ghetto, profanity is an enviable talent. It is to be fine tuned and practiced as often as necessary. Since most poor people feel a deep sense of powerlessness, profanity is a form of "ghetto power." The idea being, what have I got to lose by using profanity? In many instances, it gets you what you want-respect. Those who curse loudly and liberally are respected and held in high esteem in ghettos. It's something about those vulgarities that pour adrenalin into the bloodstream. Most of the words I heard Ruby Red say were malicious and despicable. The manner in which she spoke to her children was abominable. When she had visitors, there would be a surge of bitch, muthafucka, sons of bitches, shit, goddamn and more, most invectives hurled at her children.

However, being a new resident of this hellhole titled Parkside Homes; I decided it was in my best interest to make friends with such a "powerful" person. She hailed from a large and seemingly loving family. Ruby had six brothers. They were very protective of her and the children. The brothers never interested me sexually, intellectually or otherwise. These men frightened me and for the sake of safety, I knew it was in my best interest to establish a friendship with Ruby Red. This was a blessing in disguise. It was also my ticket to peace in the projects. I knew I lived next door to fools. I decided to make the most of it.

Although I was sleeping on the floor, had one change of clothes, begging for diapers, using the food pantry, unable to afford a phone and begging the Salvation Army for a Christmas voucher, I considered myself better that Ruby Red. How absurd!

I always spoke to Ruby Red and her guests. These were derelicts, the wretched of the earth. Nothing but drunks and dope fiends frequented her abode. Their revelries lasted from early morning to early morning. It didn't matter what they were talking about; I made it my point to speak. I made eye contact. I smiled. I shared and even borrowed food from Ruby Red. Soon my efforts began to pay off. I'd become part of the "group." I no longer feared robberies, breakends, rape or other forms of abuse. I roamed that huge project without fear. Ruby and I were neighbors for several years. She moved after her application for Section Eight was approved.

NEW QUARTERS
12/7/92

Thank you Higher Power for your grace and mercy. The last leg of my drunkenness almost landed me in the penitentiary. On an annual basis or as requested by the manager of the facility, the federal government required residents of Parkside Homes to provide proof of income. Dayton City Schools hired me as a full-time educator in August 1989. Because of my increased income, I was given an ultimatum. Very simply, I was to leave Parkside Homes or begin paying a monthly rental rate of $600.00 for my roach-infested apartment of over fifteen years. Parkside was my incubator, my protector.

My Alabama / Brooklyn existence was one of a child-vagabond with its accomplice- sexual molestation. My Cleveland existence was one of frustration and intolerance with its co-conspirators- my sick family. Kent State was my period of limbo and uncertainty. I was running in the fast lane blindfolded. My death would surely have happened if my daughter weren't conceived. Parkside was my first real home in twenty years. When we moved there, I felt a sense of relief. I knew I'd get my life together in Parkside. Yes, Parkside was a giant stepping stone. It was my temporary heaven in hell. Now, it was time to leave Parkside. I was afraid.

It took only a few days to find a place. The freeway was a stone's throw from my new home, Lantern Arms. A municipal park was across the street. I moved to the sixth floor, just below the penthouse. I could see downtown Dayton from my patio window. I could see for miles. My new home was clean on the outside. Inside, it was infested with whores, crime, drugs, confusion, chaos and malice. The same vermin I thought I'd left in Parkside. Unlike the rowhouses of Parkside, these apartments were stacked on top of the other. In short, I moved into a vertical Parkside. I was still drinking and drugging and soon became a willing participant in the continuous mischief and mayhem.

Lantern Arms was owned by a slumlord lawyer. When I moved in, it was managed by a hillbilly who'd adopted black boys and permitted their criminal activities. This hillbilly was smart. He had enough sense to know his skinny, old, wrinkled, white, chain smoking ass couldn't manage drunks, whores, druggies, etc, without turning a deaf ear and getting his cut. His adoptees were drug pushers. They paid him to oversee their business transactions. It was rumored he was a crackhead and his "boys" supplied his habit.

I was sexually unsatisfied and still dating my married sugardaddy. I needed a lover. I'd train him to satisfy my sexual appetites. He too lived on the sixth floor. We were practically across the hall from one another. Please understand since I can remember I always selected men based upon fear, protection or financial gain. Never in life, even now, have I considered the "right" reasons. Circumstances in my life have dictated I be in control of my man. No matter how I treat him he's to do what I want.

Folks there are no secrets in the lives of drunks and dope fiends. Our objective at all times is selfish and self-centered. This philosophy changes when one becomes tired of living like a beast, an animal. When I moved to Lantern

Arms, I was not tired. I was prone to deceive and to deception. I was ripe for what was to happen. It happened in Lantern Arms. My wheeling and dealing caused great harm to myself and others. Please understand it takes two to tango. The other half involved in this tangled web of lies and deception was also a drunk and druggie. My desire for sexual pleasure was the root cause of this inevitable tragedy.

THE SHOOTING
12/7/92

My sugardaddy didn't satisfy me sexually. He was a ninety second man. I wouldn't have dared end our relationship because of something as simple as sex. The money given to me by this man represented power and control. My basic needs for food, clothing, shelter, booze and plenty of my wants, at the time, were supplied by him. He was staying and I was playing.

The new playmate was chosen without prudence or judicious introspection. This man worked for Goodwill Industries and according to rumor, was emotionally unbalanced. Although not an employee of Goodwill Industries, I was certainly just as emotionally unstable as he was. His name was Marvin M. As with earlier triangles, there was bound to be trouble. It wasn't long in coming. I lied to Marvin about everything. I lied to him about my drinking and drug habit. I lied to him about the other man. The Iceman also known as the sugardaddy was frequenting my apartment on a nightly basis. When the sugardaddy was over and Marvin would knock, I'd pretend not to be in. My spiteful neighbors would assure him I was home.

Things escalated and Marvin became violent. A push here, a shove there, before you knew it, we were fighting on a regular basis. I'd whip his skinny ass. You're already aware of my fear of men. I'd choose short, skinny men because I could beat them. If they fucked with me, their ass belonged to me. So it went with Marvin. It wasn't enough to kick his ass. I had to fight him time and again. I believe he enjoyed getting beat up.

After a few of weeks of this madness, I said "enough." This was crazy and I wasn't going to be a part of it anymore. I told Marvin to get out of my life and leave me the fuck alone. Instead, Marvin kept harassing me. I called the apartment manager. He talked with Marvin. The harassment continued. I called the police they talked with Marvin. All efforts proved futile. It happened in the spring of 1991.

Marvin kicked my apartment door in and attacked me. I again called the police who as usual arrived after the fact. The manager claimed he'd repair the door as soon as possible. I filed charges, but by this time Marvin had disappeared. The police left with their reports from the manager, neighbors and me. Later that afternoon, Marvin returned.

He was intoxicated and angry. Before going into his apartment, he stood in the hallway and loudly threatened me. I heard him slam his door. I left my apartment in fear. I immediately went to the golf course and shared the day's events with the Iceman. He listened intently and inquired about my safety. Since he was married, I knew his involvement was limited. However, once I talked with the Iceman, I felt better. As long as I followed my rental agreement, I had a right to my apartment. I was going home.

The drive from the golf course was short, less than fifteen minutes. Thank God, I was sober. At the time, I was driving my long, yellow Cadillac; I'd fittingly named "Sunshine." As I parked Sunshine and walked through the apartment lobby, I felt uneasy and nervous.

The elevator was repaired earlier in the day so I didn't take the steps to my sixth floor apartment. As I stepped into it, I prayed Marvin was gone. Immediately upon returning from the golf course, I'd placed my bicycle against the door for support. The hinge and door locks were already busted loose from his kicking. I'd been in my apartment less than five minutes and then it happened. He began kicking the already broken door, cursing and loudly exclaiming he was going to "fuck me up!" I shot to my bedroom and grabbed my gun from the dresser drawer. The bike hit the floor with a loud 'thud'. Marvin rushed towards me, ranting and raving coming towards me. He said he wasn't going to jail. His eyes were filled with hate and rage.

I was on the phone trying to reach the police when he charged me. I dropped the phone and pointed the weapon and fired. He ran out of the apartment screaming. I was in close pursuit, still firing the pistol. He ran down the back staircase. I was on his heels. He was hit twice. He collapsed on the third floor, in front of the apartment manager's door.

As he laid there with the barrel of a Smith and Wesson thirty-eight less that a foot from his brain, a voice said "don't do it." It seemed I took forever deciding whether or not to send his soul to heaven or to hell. I wasn't God. In short the decision took only a split second. As he lay there, I cursed and kicked him. He was bleeding profusely. All the fear had dissipated and a sense of calm now enveloped me. I felt at peace. I felt relieved. I moved the gun barrel away from his head. I walked the three flights to the sixth floor. The police were on their way. The manager's slave-sons also called them.

I placed the gun near the patio, far away from me and the couch, but visible to the police when they arrived. I sat on the couch in my sixth floor apartment and looked at my Associate and Bachelor's degrees. The shooting was in self defense, yet I wondered about my sentence. I envisioned penitentiary cell bars closing around me. What a fucking waste. All the years of clawing and scraping were for what!? I waited. I didn't have long to wait. The door was already off its hinges so there was no need to knock. A big, burly, black cop was first on the scene, followed by a white officer in a white shirt. I assumed he was the superior officer. The two were followed by the manager and curious onlookers. The black policeman asked no questions. He immediately cuffed me. The apartment manager informed the police of Marvin's previous actions. They were told of the incident which occurred earlier in the day and that charges were already in the works against Marvin. Neighbor's told of Marvin's nightly harassment and our nearly daily screaming and fighting matches.

I remained on the couch, handcuffed throughout the interrogation. I answered all questions in a quiet subdued manner. After the interrogation was over, the white officer told his subordinate to remove the cuffs. This he did without question or hesitation. They left. Alone and confused, I replayed the actions which led to the shooting.

Again, alcohol was unmasked. During the "courtship" Marvin brought me plastic flowers. He gave me a few dollars here and there. We took walks together. We drank and did drugs together. He too was a lousy lover. Ours was a typical alcoholic liaison. Alcohol controlled the relationship from beginning to end. Everything about the relationship was superficial. Underneath it rage, anger and guilt fought for center stage. Thank you Higher Power for sobriety today. Please protect me and keep me safe.

Marvin spent several days hospitalized. Afterwards, he did six months in the workhouse. I neither called nor visited. I was through with him. The day he was released, my Cadillac was vandalized. I never found out who did it, but I had my suspicions. A few days later, I received a threatening call from Marvin. I called his mama. I called his brother, who was a police officer in another jurisdiction. I placed calls to Dayton's police department. Marvin received a year's probation because of the threatening phone calls. There are times when I am out and about and I will see Marvin. We don't speak. He is someone I can live without. God thank you.

PILLS, PILLS, PILLS
12/8/92

Today I am booze and dope free. Why are my thoughts digressing to1984? This was the year I first became involved with twelve groups. My frenzied mind convinced me all I needed to do was put down the booze. The weed and pills were alright. So, I put down the booze. I was "dry." I began to voraciously ingest dry drugs like Tylenol #3's, Xanex, Valium, Black Beauties, 714's, Percodan, Percocet, Somas, etc- an orchestra of deadly drugs. My body had a high tolerance for drugs. I would take three Tylenol #3's, Xanex and three or four Somas over a two to three hour period and still walk. I acted really stupid though. I thought that sort of self-debauchery was cute. My mind told me I was the one of the best pill poppers in town. How sick!! Everywhere I went, bootleg joints, private homes, nightclubs, I'd be high off of pills.

Pills, pills, pills were coming out of my ears and ass. I still wasn't getting the hazy, crazy, out of control "high" alcohol always provided. I had a soul sickness and the pill high couldn't ease the pain like booze. I was fully functional on pills and rarely caused trouble. I needed more!

Booze was always followed by blackouts and outlandish behavior. Whatever I imagined sober, I did drunk. I thought being drunk was the greatest thing in the world. It was 1984, I was thirty years old. My only aspiration in life was to get drunk. At age thirty, I'd earned two degrees. I was working part-time as a substitute teacher. I had a beautiful daughter. I hated myself and life. It was only a matter of time before I went back to the bottle. Thank you God for the gift of sobriety. Thanks so much!

I GIVE
12/8/92

Initially I wouldn't permit any twelve step program to work in my life. The reason being I wasn't ready to "quit." I hadn't hurt myself enough. I hadn't lost everything. However, when I darkened the door of recovery for round two, I was ready. I was beat. The second time around proved to be my saving grace. Booze was a formidable foe. I couldn't beat it without help. In October, 1991, I no longer cared to win. I needed help. I'm glad God gave me a second chance at life.

Today my twelve step program is simple. It's designed to set me free from my self-imposed prison. I am the one who complicates it. I'd built thick impenetrable prison walls around me. I constructed the walls as defenses against the arrows, bombardments and gashes of life. I built the walls to protect me from the pain of love. I built the walls to protect me from the pain of the childhood rapes and molestations. I built them to protect me from remembering the neglect and cruelty of my unfeeling and seemingly unloving mama. They were built to protect me from searing pain of the desertion of my daughter's father. There were constructed to protect my alcohol and drug addiction, because in reality, none of the earlier circumstances turned me into an alcoholic. **I became alcoholic simply because I drank too much alcohol.**

The booze and dope walls crumbled when Joshua in the guise of my Higher Power blew his mighty horn. My tarnished soul began to shine. If you are a real alcoholic or dope fiend, you must stop drinking and start believing in another power greater than yourself- a **spiritual power**.

CONTRIBUTIONS
12/8/92

Where do parents fit in this tangled web? Parents are our first caregivers. These are the people we first love. We love them even before ourselves. Our basic needs of food, clothing and shelter, are usually supplied by our parents. As I grew, I thought it was morally righteous to hang onto previous hurts and upsetting childhood traumas.

Alcoholics and drug abusers are irresponsible. We use every excuse imaginable to deny acceptance and responsibility for our drunkenness. We blame our parents for all our failures and thus shift responsibility away from ourselves. I blamed mama.

In sobriety I am responsible for my actions-all of them. I release anger through positive outlets. Today, I use speaking, writing, dancing, singing, exercise, cursing, proper nutrition and meditation as outlets. In sobriety, I seek peace inwardly by challenging my belief system on a daily system. The challenge is to grow up psychologically and become a contributor to this great society. Contributor you say, well there were plenty of drunks and dope fiends who've contributed to this great society. You're right-but I'm talking about us-you and me. What are we going to do on a daily basis which will aid mankind's growth and development?

I am writing books and speaking across the country. What are you doing? I hope it's thinking about your life. Only human beings are blessed with the ability to think. Through critical thinking and positive action, in time we outgrow some immaturity. We learn to live with abandon and freedom, away from our self-imposed penitentiaries. We learn to give of ourselves.

For drunks and dope fiends, sobriety is the key. Sobriety is the key!! **You don't need a twelve step program either. They're what I used and still use today, they aren't**

mandatory. It's just easier if you're involved with a twelve step group.

The belief in a Higher Power is a must. For years my Higher Power was booze and drugs. Today, I believe and have faith in a Power greater than Queen. This Power can't be touched, seen, tasted, smelled or felt. It is revealed through interaction with others who need my help. Just accept there is a Power greater than alcohol and drugs. It's time to come in out of the rain. Let your sun shine.

What's your interpretation of the pictures?

_____

_____

_____

_____

_____

_____

_____

_____

_____

KIDS
12-9-92

Sometimes I wonder why I care these days. Drunks and dope fiends seem a cowardly lot. They're always looking for a quick fix and an easy way out. They are shame-based and guilt ridden. They're forever inventing excuses for their destructive behaviors. They are pitiful. There are times I wish they'd just disappear from the earth. They wreak so much havoc within the society. They're the worst scavengers.

As an educator I see the poisoned tentacles of drunks and junkies suck the life blood from their children. These children for the most part, love and adore them. Their children will come to hate them if the decadence continues. Their children want to do right but are sabotaged because their parents lust for alcohol and drugs. Their children have babies trying to compensate for the lack of love in the home.

The child's personality is fragile. It's also the part of the psyche that's the strongest, most vulnerable and most creative. It must be reckoned with. Adult killers, rapists, thieves, and women batterers are many times the products of alcoholic and abusive households during childhood. For some, these forms of soul sickness are hidden by money and material goods, yet the truth always surfaces.

I look at sobriety as my resurrection from the dead. Not the resurrection we are conditioned to believe in. My resurrection didn't occur over a period of three days, I'm resurrected daily. Each morning I wake up sober, I'm experiencing a "resurrection." All societies since creation have had their share of alcoholics and drug addicts. I'm not talking about those societies. I'm talking about this one. The one that's scandalously raped and robbed on a daily basis. The great society that masks its decadence by pretending everything is fine and dandy. For instance, let's look at my daughter.

She started having problems and concerns before elementary school. One night, I wanted to get drunk and left her over a bitch's house. The bitch had a son. He was seven or eight years of age. We returned early and caught her son fucking my daughter. Now a real woman would have sat down with the boy's mother and talked about the bullshit.

No, I yelled and screamed at my daughter. She was only four years old. I was totally unfit. I couldn't protect my own four year old daughter. I was blinded by denial, alcoholism, self-hatred and a real need to destroy myself. Please forgive me dear daughter. Queen, please forgive yourself. Throughout my daughter's elementary school years, I ignored the signs of my alcoholism. Yet my booze and drug habit always took center stage to everything. Always!!!

Children make many mistakes. I wasn't allowed to make mistakes without severe punishments. If my daughter made simple mistakes, I would beat her. I was a clone of my sick drunken mother. Are you? Same old story-a very old and sad story. If you've been through enough self-inflicted pain, this book will help you. It not, it may still benefit you. Today you know your concern and you know how to get help.

Jamessa was named after her father with the "sa" from Teresa added at the end. She made her entrance into the world of her mother's alcoholism on October 12, 1974, at 2:18p.m. What a healthy baby. My daughter weighed eight pounds four ounces and was twenty-one inches long. She was born at St. Elizabeth's Hospital in Dayton, Ohio. Today they call it St Elizabeth's Medical Center. Since I'd been in labor twenty-two hours, I told her father to go to work that October afternoon. I didn't really want him to go to work, but he went anyway. In my heart, I wanted James to say "no"-"I'm with you from beginning to end." This was the birth of our baby. As a result of my playing "superwoman," hospital personnel, in essence strangers, were my sole comforters during what should have been the happiest day of my twenty year existence. If you're pregnant and want your baby's father with you throughout labor and delivery, let him know.

It's the least he can do, especially if you aren't married.

Playing superwoman is another of those carryovers from slavery. You can research that on your own. In the meantime, take my word for it, it is. I left James in the spring of 1975, a year after the Xenia, Ohio tornado. Our relationship had collapsed. Either he was drunk or I was. Our daughter was well taken care of though. My daughter was breastfed during the first six months of her life. She was healthy and strong. She never had a diaper rash or cold during infancy and toddlerhood.

After our breakup, I returned to Cleveland. For three or four weeks, I worked for the county board of elections. Former Cleveland businessman, Saul Stillman was responsible for my getting that job. In my ignorance, I had no idea of the future and stability a "county" job provided. My ghetto sense of security, life and happiness, looked at "working" as the slow road to riches and wealth. Since most movie stars were whores, who made it big, I tried prostitution. I quit my county job and started dancing in a bar called the "Bedroom" on the corner of East 105th and Euclid. This was a known hangout for prostitutes, pimps, drug addicts, gamblers and criminals of all sorts. Initially, I loved this quagmire of human filth.

THE PIMP
12/9/92

My baby's father and I drank too much together and there was always trouble. When I left him, I took only my baby. A former Kent State girlfriend, Belita T. S. allowed my daughter and me to reside with her in Cleveland. She also introduced me to two elderly ladies who cared for my daughter while I ran the streets. I had relatives in Cleveland, however, we weren't close. I resided briefly with an aunt, but since I no longer wanted to abide by her rules, I moved out.

My attitude and booze had driven a wedge between us.

The pimp's name was Chuck. I met him the first night of go-go dancing. He was everything the ghetto conditioned me to want in a shit-hole of a man. He had missing teeth and those that remained were in need of a toothbrush, floss and professional attention. Unless he opened his mouth, one would consider him handsome. A pimp is a conman. Chuck was a con artist and I wanted to be conned. Pimps remind me of vultures. They carefully choose weak prey. They feed on the dead and dying souls of hurt human beings. I was dying inside and ripe for whoredom. The first thing they do is "qualify" a potential whore. If there's a family rift or other negative concerns, he'll sense the neediness. If she's unaccustomed to kindness, she will respond to the smallest acts of kindness with gratitude and obedience. For a few days he'll treat her well. He'll listen (they're fantastic listeners) to cries of "woe is me." This signals to him she's the right one. Nine times out of ten, if she works in a nude or semi-nude bar, she'll eventually become a whore. Lastly, a good pimp will trick a whore into thinking she is smarter than he is. The pimp pits his wits against hers. He soon moves in for the kill.

In my particular circumstances, the "kill" happened this way. The two or three day rendezvous was over. During the day, I worked for the Board of Elections. At night I danced in the bar. I was seeing less and less of my baby and I missed her. It took about two weeks before I quit my solid county job. A week later, I quit my dancing job. The money I'd earned from both jobs, I gave to the pimp. My daughter got nothing.

My baby was cared for by strangers. I was sleeping on a stinking couch. I was embarrassed by the label "whore" and wouldn't walk the corners in the day. My wife-in-law would work the triple X theatres and I started working them too.

My county job paid decent money. My dancing job

paid $400 a week. I exchanged all of this for a snaggled tooth, needle popping piece of carrion. Thank you Higher for sobriety today. The "good" in me wanted out of the whore racket. A woman takes care of her babies and herself before she spends a penny on a junkie muthafuckin' niggah. Besides that, pimps are timid. They need vulnerable women to validate their scavenger like existence. They really don't like women, not even their mothers. The exploitation of women is an act of revenge. They are getting even with the mama who neglected and / or abused them.

I wanted out of this racket and told him so. The wife-in-law was with us. The three of us were sitting on a ragged, smelly and dilapidated bed. He listened intently. I talked about how my baby needed me. I talked about the gossip that was rampant in my family regarding by behavior. I talked about my dreams and goals. Suddenly, out of nowhere came a fist-POW! I was dazed. He asked me who I thought I was lying to him that way. A foot came up and landed on my knee. Each punch was followed by a "speech." This "speech" supposedly justified his brutality. After it was over, my lip was busted and bleeding. My eyes and knees were swollen. I ached all over. This wasn't what I'd planned.

Soon after beating me, he "shot up," and went into a nod. The wife-in-law did the same. I wasn't sure if they were sleep, so I didn't do anything. From my stinking couch, I could see them sprawled over the bed. It seems I watched them for hours. They never changed positions. I'd been away from my baby all day. It was now after eleven o'clock p.m. I was stiff and the slightest movement brought tears. The pain was intensifying. Why in hell did I permit this? I had a high school diploma and a little college. I wasn't going to punk out in whoredom. Tears caused by guilt, pain and shame began to trickle down my cheeks.

Another hour passed and the two bodies remained in

a drug-induced sleep. This time, the wife-in-law was resting on her side. He was as he'd been for the last few hours. I sat up on the couch. Johnny Carson was on. Although paralyzed with fear, I knew I had to act. My clothes were in a back room of the apartment. I had to get away.

All the money I'd earned over the past weeks went into his veins. There was no way I was going to whore for a junkie muthafucka. The son of a bitch beat my ass, because I changed my mind about becoming a street whore. Where was my mind? What self-destructive forces were operating inside me? Why did I even remotely consider streetwalking? These thoughts and more raced through my mind as I contemplated the distance from the couch to the door.

"Get up and get out!" I decided to act. With only my bra and panties, I tiptoed to the door. My breathing was shallow and my heartbeat seemed loud enough to wake them. Still, I inched toward the door, opened it and vanished. As I hopped the six flights of steps two by two, I imagined bullets whizzing past my head. I'd die and go to hell before I'd live in this *hell* called whoredom. How wrong I was. Upon reaching the ground, I raced to the nearby police station.

The station was but a couple of blocks from the pimp's apartment. I bolted through the front door with terror written over my countenance. Even then, my Higher Power was watching over me. A white officer eyed me from behind the counter. He knew what had happened. It was an old story. Yet and still, I relayed each dark and gory detail of the incident in the apartment. He listened and did nothing. I said I wanted to press charges. He totally ignored those words and asked whether I needed to use the telephone.

I called my alienated Aunt Nell. She in turn called my Uncle Arthur. Within an hour they were both by my side. I was

whisked away covered by my aunt's housecoat. It was so humiliating. Yet, this was not the final straw.
Describe a situation in which a law enforcement officer may have saved your life.

_____

_____

_____

_____

_____

_____

_____

_____

_____

RETURN TO DAYTON
12/9/92

James, Jamessa's father drove from Dayton to Cleveland and picked us up. Within a week's time, I'd left again. There was no way I would endure the emotional anguish any longer. My daughter and I stayed with friendly strangers for a few days. I'd applied for subsidized housing in the spring of 1975, a few months before the Cleveland fiasco.

On December 17, 1975, my fourteen month old daughter and I moved into Parkside Homes. This liaison would remain intact for over fifteen years. Within this period, I'd earned two college degrees, lose custody of my daughter and live through some of the worst bouts with alcoholism imaginable. Time after time, alcohol would literally rip me to shreds. It is only by the grace of a loving God that I'm able to share a pittance of my many tales with you. It is my hope that you will grasp a few of these poignant words and hold on for dear life.

As a young mother, I doted on education. It had been purported as the way out for ghetto niggahs. Ladies and gentlemen, boys and girls, that's the honest truth. Education does make a difference. For me, college life was sterile and initially boring. Most professors taught theory. I integrated my street knowledge with my college experiences.

The smartest students were the nerds and geeks. They still are. These same nerds and geeks are running this world today. Take a hard cold and calculated look around you. Ghetto pimps, players, whores, drunks, dope fiends and petty cons are habitually in and out of jail. The nerd or geek can rob the nation blind and never do a single day behind bars.

Check it out! Take that sterile college existence and fertilize it with your personal pack of street manure. Regrettably, I can't save anybody who doesn't want to be saved. The key to motivation is provide the stimulus and the individual will decide upon the response. Alcoholics are prime examples of how an avalanche works. If they're still using, one drink is all it takes for the snowball effect.

Describe nerds or geeks you know.

_____

_____

_____

_____

_____

_____

_____

_____

_____

_____

_____

SCHOOL PROM
12/9/92

For some odd reason, thoughts of my high school prom are racing through my head. Throughout my junior and senior years, I was fortunate enough to have had a job with what used to be called OWE (Occupational Work Experience). I was assigned to the Brecksville, Ohio Veterans' Administration Hospital. Every Saturday morning, I'd board a bus from downtown Cleveland to the VA hospital. I saved my money. My mother wasn't interested in my prom, let alone buying a prom dress.

It was a yellow mini dress. Six or eight pill box buttons decorated the midline and ran vertically from collar to hem. I thought it was a beautiful dress. My figure has always been absolutely smashing. I made that sunflower yellow dress sing. My high school boyfriend had to work that night. I caught the bus and attended my high school prom alone.

I drank heavily that evening. I've even forgotten what sort of booze I ingested. At the time, 1971, "Maddog" was the rage. My guess is I drank a lot of that. Today, it's "Reddog." A dog is a dog, they bite when misused. I remember arriving at the school's gymnasium. All the girls had dates. I sat in a corner and greedily gulped the spiked punch. Before I knew what hit me; I was in an alcoholic blackout. To this day, I have no memory of that fateful night.

I was a two year varsity cheerleader. I'd lettered in track and cheerleading. Yet, I was too scared to get a fuckin' date for my once-in-a lifetime high school prom. Before mama's untimely death, before meeting my daughter's father, before the birth of my daughter, alcoholic seeds were sprouting like weeds. Maybe at my next high school reunion, I'll inquire about what happened. I'm sure one of my former classmates remembers. Who knows maybe I'll get lucky and hear the entire story. Then again, it's best if forgotten. I know I made a complete ass out of myself.

What did you do the night of your prom?

_____

_____

_____

_____

_____

_____

_____

_____

_____

_____
_____
_____
_____
_____
_____
_____
_____

THE ISLEYS
12/10/92

Shortly after my arrival at Kent State, in 1971, I met the Isley Brothers. My best girlfriend drove to Kent from Ohio State and the party started. I had money from my work study job. My girlfriend, Tanya, also had work study money. A fool and her money are soon parted. The afternoon of the Isley Brothers' concert was spent shopping for booze and outfits.

Ripple, Thunderbird, 151 Rum, Maddog and Red Lady 21 were the beverages. Marijuana and Kool filter kings were the cigarettes. Mini dresses, platform shoes and large earrings were the outfits. One of my college professors turned us on to powder cocaine. I was ready! We were ready! The evening of the concert found Tanya and I in the front row. All of a sudden-BAM! Tanya and I were out of our seats; dancing as though possessed. In truth we were. Sweat poured from our lithe teenage bodies. We slithered onto the stage.

One Isley after another felt-literally our presence and didn't miss a beat. The evening quickly progressed. The younger Isleys, Marvin, Chris and Ernie were "entertained" by us. Marvin Isley asked me to accompany him to New Jersey. However, I chose James, Jamessa's soon to be father and twenty more years of wading in and out of my alcoholic hell.

In each and every human being is the fundamental belief in God. God is infinite and therefore it is difficult to attach descriptors to the word-God. In reality, descriptors aren't necessary. All that's necessary is belief. Believe there is a power greater than you. Believe that this power can and will relieve us of the obsession to booze and dope ourselves to death.

Since time immemorial, man has placed restrictions on God. This is unintentional because man is finite. He operates within finite boundaries. All civilizations have booze and drug concerns. These concerns can be addressed in the same way. Ask God for help. This help may arrive in the manner of another sober person or even a jail cell.

Faith is the key. Faith in God's never ending love and power. We'll have faith that as we work through the pain and hell of our own creation, on a daily basis, we'll remain sober. Glory to God! Thank you for sobriety today! Thank you!

I was hung over the morning following the Isley Brothers concert. The first thought I culled was-where's my car? Earlier that summer, I'd purchased a Delmont 88. That car was a gem. It never had mechanical problems. The body was great and the interior spotless. My Higher Power was working in my life even then. This was my first car. The car salesman could've ripped me off. He sold me a really nice car. It was a sharp metallic grey with black interior. Even the wheels and tires looked good.

As I dressed, I wondered where it was. Since Tanya and I traveled mostly on campus, it had to be out front. The only time I drove was when we rendezvoused at the Holiday Inn with Chris, Marvin and Ernie Isley. This "fuck party" lasted a couple of hours; afterwards, Tanya and I were off again. I know I drove to and from the hotel. I remember our lewd conversation as we compared their genitalia. I just didn't remember the damn car.

I walked it seemed for hours that morning. I questioned every student I saw. "Have you seen a grey Oldsmobile with four doors?" No, no, all answered 'no'. I was ashamed to call the campus police. In my mind they were a joke anyhow. This was fall of 1971. May 4, 1970, was a day of bloodshed at Kent State. Students who were protesting the Vietnam War were fired upon by Ohio National Guardsmen. Four lay dead in the aftermath. Those were young, white college students. White college students were murdered by white national guardsmen. Three of the four students were Jewish. The entire nation was alarmed.

Few knew of or cared to mention the black college students gunned down in the south the previous year. Same principles, same hallowed ground, but black skin color. Oh the wedge that fear and slavery drove and continues to drive between us. After the shootings, Kent State's campus security handled students with kid gloves. Security would've probably found the car had I informed them of my dilemma.

Instead, I spent an entire morning walking, questioning and searching the campus. I assumed the car was stolen. I had no auto insurance. I just accepted the fact that my car was gone. I was tired and decided to take the short cut across campus. This meant I'd approach my dormitory from the rear. There it was. The car was parked behind my dormitory. I'd spent my entire morning looking for a car which was parked in the back of the dormitory! It didn't occur to me to go to the back door of the building and look outside. If I had done this, I'd have gotten some much needed rest. The "big" party I was attending that evening required I rest. Now I'd have to grace their presence with but a few hours of sleep. I went to the party. I drank before, during and after the party. I don't remember it or what I did. I was a seventeen year old full blown alcoholic. God thank you for sobriety today.

DRUG DOCTORS
12/11/92

Even in childhood I was figure conscious. The pretty girls had all the fun. It seemed everyone poked fun at the fat ones. So it is to this day. That's one of the main reasons I majored in Health and Physical Education. I wanted to learn how to stay pretty. I learned that and a whole lot more.

At Kent State, doctors always gave me high powered drugs. All I had to do was say how I wanted to feel. The prescription would be ready in no time. So it was with my diet pills. I'd pop a pill and my appetite would disappear. I was already slim in the waist and foxy in the face-yet I wanted more. Just a few pounds less and I'd be alright. So it went. Ask for what I want was my motto. It still is. Soon, I needed something else. I felt like a rat on an exercise wheel. I was always rushing around and excited. The nervousness brought with it irritability and insomnia.

Once again I went to the campus witchdoctor. I now needed nerve pills. That pill was valium. Boy was I setting myself up. The doctor wanted peace. He was well aware of the havoc blacks had wreaked in the large ghettos nationwide. He was well aware of the students killed by the national guardsmen. He was an old doctor. He'd soon retire. Peace was now his main objective. This "peace" was achieved by keeping his patients happy. Give them what they want.

I'd drink and take valium. I'd drink and take diet pills. I'd drink until I blacked out. I didn't think I was harming myself. I wanted only to have fun. The reality of it was- I was running away from me. I was running from mama, bad men, child molesters, slavery, Cleveland, Alabama, menstruation, death, responsibility, feelings-everything. Thus my two and a half years at Kent State University were spent in blackouts and deep depression. I eventually flunked out.

Will I ever truly love me? I look around at the beautiful women who've chosen to become lesbians. What a fucking waste of pussy. If I'm to avoid this trick of the mind, I must learn to love me on a daily basis. I have to accept my femininity and all of its ramifications. To teach myself to love another woman sexually is a misnomer. It is wrong. It stems from hurt and pain caused by adults who abused helpless children.

This is a touchy subject because I thought I'd become a dyke. The rejection from my mama and the malfeasance from other significant males made me wonder. Would this rejection of my womanhood stop the pain? If I began to love women sexually, would I feel better? No! A resounding no! The only way to grasp the significance of this learned malady is to focus on Queen.

HOSTAGES
12/11/92

What do I enjoy sexually with men? What can I teach my man sexually about me? I'm learning through prayer and meditation that patience is more than virtuous, it's mandatory for alcoholics. It's a must for people in pain. People in pain, maim, kill and destroy literally everything in their path. This includes children, possessions, creativity, social morays and jobs. Pain doesn't compromise. It's like a muscle during a contraction. It's all out! Pain takes no prisoners.

People loving alcoholics and wishing them well doesn't matter. It's only through belief in God, self-acceptance and not drinking today, that slowly erodes the negative self image. We drunks bring unfortunate troubles upon ourselves. It's as though, during drunkenness, we're subconsciously saying-kill me! That's right, looking for someone, or something to put us out of our perceived misery. Most of us are too neurotic to just blow our fucking brains out. That would be too easy. We have to take hostages with us as we stagger through the corridors of our alcoholic hell. Hell is always better when we have company. Sick! Sick! Sick! **Use the lines below and journal about today's pain. Remember- you are loved, by me and by God. Use additional paper as needed.**

_____

_____

_____

_____

_____

_____

_____

_____

_____

MENSTRUATION
12/12/92

Since I'm currently menstruating, I'll talk about this natural phase of the lifecycle. We were living with my grandmother and her "tied to the apron-string" grown babies. Grandma lived in a house that was divided into three levels. It was a perfect abode for several of her grown children, my mother included. Grandma lived on the first floor. An aunt and her husband-boy and five children at that time, resided on the second floor. We made our home on the third floor also known as the "attic."

I remember this as though it happened yesterday. I had just turned twelve in the hot summer month of July. I was walking from the attic to the first floor one day and felt warm and wet between my legs. I ran my fingers across my vagina. They showed red. With my heart racing, I bolted back to the attic. I believed I'd be beat if anyone found out. I was beyond terrified. What was I to do? I didn't want "it" to run down my legs.

What was I to do? In Alabama, I'd seen Kotex and smelled Massengill's stinking yellow douche. I didn't know what they were for. I did know the Massengill of the seventies smelled like burnt sulfur. It had a horrible stench! There were no sanitary napkins. At least, I couldn't find any. Instead I found rags and tore them into rectangular strips. These were then folded and used as sanitary napkins. When these make-shift pads were saturated, I'd unfold each and wash it. I'd hang these strips out of my bedroom window and wait until they dried. In the summer heat, it wasn't a very long wait.

The smell of blood was everywhere. I know how Lady Macbeth felt during her nightly washing ritual. I was ashamed and filled with ignorance about puberty. This monthly rag ritual continued for several months.

The crime was ignorance. Mama told me nothing, neither did anyone else, male or female. I was experiencing the birth of my womanhood and totally unprepared for one of the most sacred experiences in life. In my mind, menstruation was a dirty word. This event was shrouded in myth. I vowed I'd never tell mama. Next to not knowing how women became pregnant, not telling was the epitome of denial. Then out of nowhere, pain reared its' ugly head. I had cramps! These weren't ordinary cramps! They were psychological cramps. Cramps so severe, I'd vomit and remain bedridden for two or three days a month. Cramps so violent, I'd be rushed to the hospital in an ambulance.

The emergency room doctors would inject me with high powered narcotics and prescribe Percodan, codeine and other morphine based drugs. It was only during my menstrual cycle that I was stroked in a positive way. My family, even mama, paid attention to me. Everyone felt sorry for me. I was in real pain. All throughout my junior and senior high school years, I was absent two or three days monthly. This happened every single month until my mother died.

From its' onset, my menstrual cycle has been regular as the sun's rising and setting. Unless I was pregnant, my periods were always on time. I've given birth once out of three pregnancies. I've had two abortions. These pregnancies were conceived in alcoholic blackouts. Thank God for abortions.

How do you feel about your choices thus far?

_____

_____

_____

SPEAK NO EVIL
12/13/92

In sobriety I see the world through clear eyes. I see mothers with five and six little children selling themselves and their babies for booze and dope. I see helpless, hungry and angry children. They're neglected because mama or daddy is a hopeless drunk or junkie. In my heart, I knew I had a problem. My daughter went through hell on earth. Like me she too was robbed of her innocence. Since being drunk and high were what I liked best, I'd get rid of her as often as possible.

My last babysitter was a kind and merciful woman. She was truly an angel on earth. Her name is Lillie Henry Felton. I believe she was sent to me from God on high. She was affectionately called "Aunt Lillie." Aunt Lillie would babysit Puddin' anyday, any hour, anytime I called her. She was always there for me. She still is.

Aunt Lillie also kept two young boys. They're older than my daughter. It was the oldest of these boys who raped my daughter. My daughter only told me because she was too scared to not tell. I never told my mother about any molestation. I dared not mention my being molested by Lamar, Andrew or anyone else to my mama. I didn't think she'd believe me. Worse still, she might've accused me, a seven year old baby myself of leading two grown, funky, rusty, trifling men on. In my home, children were often blamed for the actions of adults.

My mama died of a drug overdose in May, 1971. For a great many years afterwards, I had no menstrual cramps. They were a psychological defense mechanism. The cramps were ways to get positive strokes from mama.

Becoming a woman wasn't discussed in our home-ever! My grandmother was alleged to have beaten her girls when their breasts started to develop. She believed girls menstruated because of sexual contact. In my grandmother's home, everything relating to reproduction was considered evil and bad.

My grandpapa was rumored to have had a vicious temper. He was slender in build and short of stature. He'd kick my grandmother's ass for little or nothing, and then fuck her. My grandmother and her husband, my grandfather, had fifteen children. There were ten girls and five boys. Her first child was born when she was but fifteen. Let's look at the facts. In order to bear fifteen children, you have to 'fuck'. I'm not talking about making love. I'm talking about fucking. Everytime you see each other you fuck. That's the only way those two, my grandmother and grandpapa could beget fifteen children.

Use the lines below and write about family confusion and the pain it caused you.

_____

_____

_____

_____
_____
_____
_____
_____
_____
_____
_____
_____
_____
_____

BELIEVING
12/13/92

You see everything in this book is sculptured for one purpose and one purpose only. It's to help drunks and junkies come to believe in a new way of living. We are learning to live one day at a time, without the crutches. God will hold you up. Do what you know you must. Find this God within you. That's where its been all along. Believe it! God has always been with you. The Power rests within you. Through prayer and acceptance we receive Grace and sobriety. Through Grace and sobriety we reach our goals and dreams. This decision takes less than a split second. Will we live today? Will we die today? I'm living! I'm living well!

How will you trust God today!

_____
_____
_____
_____
_____

_____

_____

_____

_____

_____

_____

_____

WHISTLING AND GUSSIE LEE
12/13/92

As a young girl in Cleveland, I remember walking home from school one day. The junior high I attended in Cleveland was called Addison. The school was located on East 79th and Hough Avenue. Like most ghetto schools, it was overcrowded, understaffed and unless something life threatening happened, generally neglected by the school board. It was rumored that Cleveland's school board spent more money on Cleveland's Westside schools. Addison, an eastside school made do with crumbs from the table.

About half way home, I started to whistle. I learned to whistle from my grandpapa. He whistled like a bird. The birds stopped singing when my grandpapa whistled. The sounds were so clear, melodic and soul stirring. On this particular day during this particular walk, I'd literally hypnotized myself whistling. I arrived at 6901 Hough Avenue before I knew it.

My grandmother was in the front yard pruning her sunflowers. She cultivated the healthiest sunflowers I'd ever laid eyes on, even to this day. When I walked in the yard, she stopped, her hands flew to her hips and a scowl graced her usually peaceful countenance. "Stop that whistling gal, I heard you all the way down the road." "Gals ain't supposed to whistle." I was stunned! Whistling soothed me and I liked it. However, my grandmother's word was law. If she said I wasn't supposed to do it, then I wasn't supposed to do it!

I carried on a love-hate relationship with my grandmother. On the one hand, I loved the way she made over me because I was beautiful. On the other, I hated the way her adult children were tied to her apron strings. My mother, moreso that the others was controlled by her. Mama always felt guilty for having three illegitimate children by married men. The children of Wilma Jenny Johnson were fathered by two different married men. It was something grandmother and the rest of the siblings never forgave her for.

Hypocrites aren't worth a plug nickel. These same finger pointers were enjoying out of wedlock sex just as mama had. I didn't want grandmother fussing with my mama about my whistling, so I stopped. From that day to this, I've never produced the melodic rhythms and crisp notes of that warm, sunny afternoon. My mama was sick and crazy enough without the whistling bullshit. In my grandmother's eyes, I was a good 'gal' for heeding her warning.

So much stupid shit swirls in the minds of drunks. We make many trivial excuses for our anti-life existence. **Drunks drink because it makes us feel good!**

Drunks and junkies are very, very childish and immature. Most of us when drinking think we are sexy. Our relationships are centered on people whom we can manipulate. We don't want to think. In sobriety thinking is mandatory. We come to enjoy using our brain. The brain is this vast unchartered territory. In the average drug dependent person it can be compared to a diamond in the rough. The more it's used and polished through thinking, the more it sparkles and shines. All sorts of memories are jockeying for position in my mind today.

AGE SIX
12/14/92

I experienced my first blackout when I was but six years old. The sun was hot that day. I remember it well. Mama, her lover, David and I were over my great aunt's shack-home in Tuskegee, Alabama. Gloria, my baby sister, wasn't born. Instead of playing with the children, I kept my eyes on the adults. As a child, I loved being around grown folks. As I sat on the back porch listening and peeking in the kitchen, I heard all sorts of adult talk and laughter.

Soon, Willie B. Gilmore, mama's lover and father of my brother, David, told her it was time to go. When he said this everyone moved from the kitchen to the front porch.
Aunt Ruth's porch was home to a swing and a couple of old dilapidated chairs. I again peered into the empty kitchen. I had to check and make sure I had an all clear.

Occasionally, mama would let David and I have a swallow of beer. She drank Schlitz and Pabst Blue Ribbon beer. I knew what I was looking for. At six years old, I knew what booze was and what it did. I knew I liked it very much. A quick survey of the kitchen table was all it took. They'd left a mason jar behind. Mason jars were cheap, popular and well made glass containers used to preserve food. They were common in country homes. My family used them for canning, drinking and eating vessels.

In this particular jar were a couple of healthy swallows of moonshine. Those few swallows were all I needed. They did the job. At six years of age, I was already turning my will over to a power greater than myself. That power was booze. I was already playing a frenzied drunk. The stage was set.

When I came too, I was in bed. Who brought me home? What did I do? How long was I asleep? These questions would be answered by someone other than me.

From the bed I heard voices coming from the porch. Our shack was only one room. It stood on stacks of bricks. There was a fireplace. A sheet was used as a room divider. This sheet gave the primitive illusion of a two room dwelling. The bed I lay in was near the fireplace. Since it was summertime, the fireplace was used for mostly cooking.

All of a sudden, I wanted to fly. Despite my deep state of intoxication, I'd convinced myself I could fly. As I lay in that bed, all I could think about was flying. At six years of age, I could read. I was a superman and supergirl fan. I thought I would turn myself into supergirl. Supergirl could fly away from the poverty, beatings and abuse.

These thoughts charged me with new found energy. I walked toward the door with its' cardboard window. As I opened it, the voices stopped. All eyes were on me. Without a word, I stepped onto the creaky wooden porch. As I looked at mama and her lover, I walked to the edge of the porch and jumped. "Whee I'm supergirl" seemed to linger in the air as I hit the ground hard. I lay there breathless. I'd literally knocked the wind out of myself. I was carried back into the shack-home. The rest of that day is a blur. This incident brings into consciousness other culprits.

What do you remember about your first alcohol experience?

_____

_____

_____

_____

_____

_____

_____

CHILD RAPISTS
12/16/92

A plethora of child molesters seemed to dominate my young world. I knew my great aunt's lover, in Tuskegee, only as Mr. Mack. Although he lived with my great aunt, they slept in separate beds. Mr. Mack was a hard working man and a chronic alcoholic. He drank mostly on the weekend. He'd get so drunk he'd piss all over himself. I remember when he fell asleep in my cousin's room. He was naked from the waist down. I don't remember where the grown folks were that day. Maybe they were on the front porch. The only time my great aunt left her shack-home was to cook for white folks. Mr. Mack and I were in the house alone.

I was in my great aunt's house staring at Mr. Mack's nakedness. At age six, his wasn't the first penis I'd seen. My drunken ass mama and her lover, Willie B. Gilmore would fuck in front of my brother and me. It was as if we weren't there. They'd fuck like dogs in heat. Thus when Mr. Mack woke up and saw me starring at him, I didn't start. He pulled me to him and had me fondle his limp cold penis. Next he tried to kiss me and stick his tongue in my mouth. UGH! I still smell the stench of vomit on his breath. I still feel the coldness of his penis in my little hand.

As I write this excerpt my face is frowned. Nasty! Mr. Mack never found sobriety. He died soon after my great aunt left Tuskegee, Alabama in the early 1970's. Rumor has it he tripped and fell, smashing his drunken head against a stone.

My great aunt Gertrude had grown sons when I was a child. There was Milton, Papa, Tiny and hatchet-head Henry. He was nick-named hatchet-head because of his big, lumpy head. Here's what child molesters do. Here's how they operate. They observe the mama of the intended victim. Child molesters look for weak parents. They rarely prey upon children who have a strong protective father in the home.

Since they are cowards, they fear an ass kicking or worse. So don't wonder why I fear men? No- understand, pray and empathize. There are plenty of honorable loving men with high values. Like the child molester, they could very well reside right next door.

In sobriety we have positive options. Unlike drunkenness, where we subconsciously chose negative options like jails, institutions and death, with sobriety comes responsibility. We become willing to work at and accept life on life's terms. This is what I'm doing with men. I want to walk through my fear and truly love a man deserving of such a fantastic woman as I am.

The real question is-"do I fear men or do I fear myself?" Life is too fucking short! I've already wasted practically two decades. Loving a man is something I'm going to experience before I die. I'm going to love a man the way a woman loves. This love will transcend the fragile world of pure sexuality. Mere physical love is wonderful. It's just so limited and superficial. I'll integrate my FISEPS (financial, intellectual, sexual, emotional, physical, and spiritual) modalities with love. Our love will elevate us to a higher plane of existence. What does my track record show? Since I'm powerless over people, places and things, here's the answer. I've been taught to fear myself.

Today is a good day to be sober.

FEAR
12/17/92

Last evening, I watched a Discovery Channel program. It was all about snakes. Everything in a snake's life, from birth to death was covered. I learned something that night. Like most other fears, this fear is also learned. Looking back, I know where it started. Living in a country town could be dangerous. Animals were everywhere-especially crawling, creeping animals. Snakes, like all reptiles, like heat. We used a fireplace for both cooking and heating during cold weather.

My earliest memories of snakes occurred in Tuskegee, Alabama. The shack-home we lived in was elevated off the ground. Early one morning, I was awaken by loud noises. My pregnant mama and her lover, Gilmore were after something. Both were half drunk and fucked out. I heard wood hitting the floor. As I turned over I saw "it." "It" was a snake!

Through my child eyes, it looked ten feet long. The reptile was still moving. A few more whacks and the snake was dead. Mama picked it up with two pieces of wood. I sat up on the mattress-bed, eyes big as saucers. She brought it towards me. I screamed and jumped off of the mattress-bed. She might have chased me with it, had Gilmore not said "Wilma leave dat gal alone."

Mama had a morose sense of humor when drunk and no sense of humor when sober. She then walked out to the porch and threw the dead creature into one of several huge beds of wild unmanicured foliage. It seemed I watched that snake all day. I thought it would move. It was dead. It lay in our yard until some neighborhood kids moved it. From that day on, I purposely avoided that part of the yard.

For months afterwards, I lay awake at night- terrified. I imagined snakes crawling in my bed. They were crawling in my vagina. They were everywhere. I carefully checked the bedding before I crawled onto the mattress. The fear only worsened. Shortly after the in-house snake killing, my mama went into labor. I was seven years and three months of age that October night. I told you this book was crazy.

GLORIA

12/16/92

On the night of October 10, 1961, mama was in hard labor. David was asleep. Gilmore was home with his wife. Mama woke me up. "Go get Auntie Ruth," she groaned. "Mama I'm sleepy" was my reply. Instantly, I dropped off to sleep once again. "Go get Auntie Ruth!" Mama was crying. She was doubled over in pain. This time, I put on my pants and shirt and stepped out into the bright Tuskegee night.

It was fall. The night was clear and crisp. The fear returned. Rattlesnakes and other animals might be out hunting. From our shack-house, the dirt road was but a few feet away. As I stepped onto it, and passed other shack-houses, I knew in but a few hours, the road would be filled with the laughter and screams of children at play.

Now, each noise caused me to quicken my step. Then in the light, of the moon, I started! I saw it -a dead snake. It had been run over by a car. I remembered mama doubled over in pain. I saw her on the kitchen floor crying. I thought she was dying. I didn't know she was pregnant. I knew nothing about labor or childbirth.

I ran! Soon I was banging on Auntie Ruth's door. I was screaming- "somethin's wrong wid mama!" "Auntie Ruth somethin's wrong wid mama!" She opened the door. I bolted in! Auntie Ruth said she was having a baby. As usual, I was the first to the rescue and the last to know why. It was that night, October 10, 1961, I walked through my fear. I loved my mama. I wanted to help her. When Gloria, my new baby sister, was brought home, I was out playing. Was I thanked for going beyond the call of duty? Was I properly cared for now that I'd saved my mama's life? No! No, no one shook my hand. I wasn't hugged or made over. My table wasn't covered with the meats and vegetables my body desperately needed. I still shot sparrows with my sling shot. Auntie Ruth still fried them for me. I still ate the "red" Alabama clay dirt. This dirt was reputedly loaded with minerals.

Mama and Gilmore were soon drinking and fucking in their old manner. She'd leave the three of us now, with whoever would keep us during her debauchery. Puddin' I know how you feel. I went through a similar childhood. I wish you the best with your daughter.

My mother's sister, Thelma, was considered wealthy. She was well groomed with seemingly perfect manners. There's one in every family. She was the daughter who had succeeded. Thelma beat the odds. Her husband was Lamar Cole. Her son was Andrew Cole. I remember them well.

It was these two men, Lamar and Andrew, moreso than any others who destroyed my psyche and innocence. It was these two men who raped and treated me like a mangy dog. It was these two men whose memories and actions are etched in my subconscious forever. It was these two men who my mama trusted. It was these two men who I believe molested many guiltless children. Like elephants, little children always remember. It's these two men I eventually came to forgive- I think.

What needs changing today? Pray for sobriety first. This book is about hope and recovery. Yes, so many experiences live within me today. God bless and thank you.

EPILOGUE
NOVEMBER 11, 2004

As of this date, I am over thirteen years sober. Good luck to you. I wish I could pour my strength and knowledge into you. However, that would be futile and pointless. You wouldn't appreciate it. Like most accomplishments in life, when we work for something we appreciate it most. Work on yourself. NEVER give up on you. Don't let a vicious addiction steal your dreams. Pray for me. Remember we are sober because of the Grace of a loving and caring God. We have only a twenty four-hour reprieve. Make the most of today. Pray and have faith in the God that dwells in you. **LET THE FUN BEGIN!**

Good Luck

Received on July 4th - 2009